"When I read Lynn Nottage's work, I feel the excitement, the allure, that early cartographers must have felt; I discover these continental maps of the human psyche never before chartered on stage. Her work explores depths of humanness, the overlapping complexities of race, gender, culture and history—and the startling simplicity of desire—with a clear tenderness, with humor, with compassion."

—PAULA VOGEL, AUTHOR OF THE PULITZER PRIZE–WINNING *HOW I LEARNED TO DRIVE*

"Nottage is a writer of commanding talents—political, but not didactic, versed in irony, not afraid to interrogate history, but still accessible and tender. One of the brightest stars of contemporary American theatre."

—LISA JONES, AUTHOR OF *BULLETPROOF DIVA*

"'Mastery . . .'—How ironic that this racist, sexist, classist word so perfectly describes Lynn's rare synthesis of eloquence and theatricality. When they invent a better word to describe 'surpassing talent . . .' please append it to Lynn Nottage's name."

—LEE BREUER, FOUNDER OF MABOU MINES AND AUTHOR OF *THE GOSPEL AT COLONUS*

On *Intimate Apparel*

"The language of *Intimate Apparel* is a thing of beauty, at times approaching poetry . . . The play is a story about citizens grabbing for the same crust of bread, occasionally pulling nourishment from one another's mouths. It is a parable about sweet dreams and honeyed words that, in an instant, can turn sour."

—DARYL H. MILLER, *LOS ANGELES TIMES*

"*Intimate Apparel* is a thoughtful, affecting new play that . . . with seamless elegance . . . offers poignant commentary on an era when the cut and color of one's dress—and, of course, skin—determined whom one could and could not marry, sleep with, even talk to in public."

—CHARLES ISHERWOOD, *VARIETY*

On *Fabulation*

"Robustly entertaining comedy, *Fabulation* is a satiric tale of the humbling of a self-invented public relations diva that subverts its comic and sentimental glibness with punchy social insights and the firecracker snap of unexpected humor."

—BEN BRANTLEY, *NEW YORK TIMES*

"I'm not sure if Lynn Nottage is two or three—or more!—playwrights. This exceptionally gifted playwright, the same storyteller who wrote the tragic *Intimate Apparel*, has written a lighthearted social comedy this time around. *Fabulation* is a wry satire (or moral fable), yet it connects to the unmistakable compassion and class struggle of the tragic *Intimate Apparel*."

—JOHN HEILPERN, *NEW YORK OBSERVER*

"After Nottage has her say, you'll never look at female prison inmates, young black mothers, or bureaucratic officials quite the same way. She has a keen knack for uncovering real human truth while never ignoring the often too-visible outward sheen of absurdity. That's a big part of what makes *Fabulation* work."

—LINDA WINER, *NEWSDAY*

INTIMATE APPAREL

FABULATION

INTIMATE APPAREL

FABULATION

or The Re-Education of Undine

LYNN NOTTAGE

THEATRE COMMUNICATIONS GROUP
NEW YORK
2006

This publication is made possible in part with public funds from the New York State Council on the Arts, a State Agency.

TCG books are exclusively distributed to the book trade by Consortium Book Sales and Distribution.

LIBRARY OF CONGRESS CATALOGING-IN-PUBLICATION DATA

Nottage, Lynn
Intimate apparel ; and, Fabulation, or The re-education of Undine / Lynn Nottage.
—1st ed.
p. cm.
ISBN: 978-1-55936-279-5
ISBN-10: 1-55936-279-0
1. African Americans—Drama. I. Nottage, Lynn. Fabulation, or, The re-education of Undine. II. Title: Fabulation, or, The re-education of Undine. III. Title: Re-education of Undine. IV. Title: Fabulation. V. Title.
PS3564.O795I58 2006
812 .54—dc22
2006006830

Book design and composition by Lisa Govan
Cover art and design by Mark Melnick

First Edition, September 2006
Fifth Printing, October 2018

For Tony

CONTENTS

INTIMATE APPAREL

PRODUCTION HISTORY

Intimate Apparel was commissioned and first produced by South Coast Repertory (David Emmes, Producing Artistic Director; Martin Benson, Artistic Director; Paula Tomei, Managing Director) in Costa Mesa, California and CENTERSTAGE (Irene Lewis, Artistic Director; Michael Ross, Managing Director) in Baltimore, Maryland opening on April 18, 2003. It was directed by Kate Whoriskey; the set design was by Walt Spangler, the costume design was by Catherine Zuber, the lighting design was by Scott Zielinski, the sound design was by Lindsay Jones, the original music was by Reginald Robinson; the arranger and piano coach was William Foster McDaniel; the dramaturg was Jerry Patch and the stage manager was Randall K. Lum. The cast was as follows:

ESTHER	Shané Williams
MRS. DICKSON	Brenda Pressley
MRS. VAN BUREN	Sue Cremin
MR. MARKS	Steven Goldstein
MAYME	Erica Gimpel
GEORGE	Kevin Jackson

Intimate Apparel was originally produced in New York City by the Roundabout Theatre Company (Todd Haimes, Artistic Director; Ellen Richard, Managing Director), opening on April 8, 2004. It was directed by Daniel Sullivan; the set design was by Derek McLane, the costume design was by Catherine Zuber, the lighting design was by Allen Lee Hughes, the sound design was by Marc Gwinn. Original music was by Harold Wheeler and the stage manager was Amy Patricia Stern. The cast was as follows:

ESTHER	Viola Davis
MRS. DICKSON	Lynda Grávatt
MRS. VAN BUREN	Arija Bareikis
MR. MARKS	Corey Stoll
MAYME	Lauren Velez
GEORGE	Russell Hornsby

CHARACTERS

ESTHER, African American, thirty-five
MRS. DICKSON, African American, fifties
MRS. VAN BUREN, white, American, thirties
MR. MARKS, Romanian Orthodox Jewish immigrant, thirties
MAYME, African American, thirty
GEORGE, Barbadian immigrant, thirties

TIME

1905

PLACE

Lower Manhattan

PRODUCTION NOTE

The set should be spare to allow for fluid movement between the various bedrooms. The action should flow seamlessly from scene to scene. The act endings mark the only true blackouts in the play.

 # Act One

Scene i

Wedding Corset: White Satin with Pink Roses

Lower Manhattan, 1905. A bedroom. It is simple, unadorned with the exception of beautifully embroidered curtains and a colorful, crazy quilt. A clumsy ragtime melody bleeds in from the parlor. In the distance the sound of laughter and general merriment. Esther, a rather plain thirty-five-year-old African American woman, sits at a sewing machine table, diligently trimming a camisole with lace. She is all focus and determination.

MRS. DICKSON *(Offstage):* Don't be fresh, Lionel. I know your mama since before the war.

(Mrs. Dickson, a handsome, impeccably groomed African American woman of fifty, enters laughing.)

There you are. Mr. Charles was admiring the bread pudding and I told him that our Esther made it. It seems he has a sweet tooth.

ESTHER: Mr. Charles is overly generous, come—the pudding ain't nothing special.

MRS. DICKSON: And did I mention that our most available Mr. Charles was promoted to head bellman at just about the finest hotel in New York? Yes.

ESTHER: But he still fetching luggage.

MRS. DICKSON: Not just any luggage, high-class luggage.

ESTHER: And is high-class luggage easier to carry?

MRS. DICKSON: I reckon it is easier to haul silk than cotton, if you know what I'm saying. *(Laughs)* And he sporting a right smart suit this evening.

ESTHER: Yes, it cashmere.

MRS. DICKSON: You can tell more about a man by where he shops, than his practiced conversation. 'Cause any man who's had enough tonic can talk smooth, but not every man has the good sense to shop at—

ESTHER AND MRS. DICKSON: Saperstein's.

(Esther laughs. Mrs. Dickson examines the embroidery on the camisole.)

MRS. DICKSON: Lovely.

ESTHER: It's for Corinna Mae's wedding night.

MRS. DICKSON: Don't tell me you've been in here all evening? Corinna Mae is getting ready to leave with her fiancé.

ESTHER: I wish I could find my party face. It really is a lovely affair. You done a fine job.

MRS. DICKSON: Come now, it ain't over yet. Put aside your sewing and straighten yourself up. There. You'll have a dance before this evening's out.

ESTHER: Please, Mrs. Dickson, I can't, really. I'll just stand there like a wallflower.

MRS. DICKSON: Nonsense, I've danced a half a dozen times, and my feet are just about worn out.

ESTHER: If I had your good looks I'd raise a bit of dust myself. Ain't nobody down there interested in me.

MRS. DICKSON: Esther, you're being silly. You've been moping around here for days. What's the matter?

ESTHER: If you must know, I turned thirty-five Thursday past.

(A moment.)

MRS. DICKSON: Oh Lord, I forgot, child. I sure did. Look at that. With Corinna Mae carrying on and all these people, it slipped my mind. Happy birthday, my sweet Esther. *(Gives Esther a big hug)*

ESTHER: It's fine. You had all this to prepare for. And I been living in this rooming house for so long, I reckon I'm just another piece of furniture.

MRS. DICKSON: Never. You were a godsend when you come to me at seventeen. Yes. I remember thinking how sweet and young you was with a sack full of overripe fruit, smelling like a Carolina orchard.

ESTHER: And now? Twenty-two girls later, if you count Lerleen. That's how many of these parties I have had to go to and play merry. I should be happy for them, I know, but each time I think, Why ain't it me? Silly Corinna Mae, ain't got no brain at all, and just as plain as flour.

MRS. DICKSON: Your time will come, child.

ESTHER: What if it don't? Listen to her laughing. God forgive me, but I hate her laughter, I hate her happiness. And I feel simply awful for saying so. And I'm afraid if I go back in there, she'll see it all over my face—and it's her day.

MRS. DICKSON: There are a number of young men open to your smile. A sour face don't buy nothing but contempt. Why our Mr. Charles has had three servings of your bread pudding.

ESTHER: And he shouldn't have had any. *(Laughs)* He weighs nearly as much as your horse.

MRS. DICKSON: Nonsense. He weighs more than poor Jessup. Shhh. He is a good man, poised for success. Yes.

ESTHER: But he's been coming to these parties for near two years and if he ain't met a woman, I'd bet it ain't a woman he after. I've been warned about men in refined suits. But still, Esther would be lucky for his attention, that's what you thinking. Well, I ain't giving up so easy.

MRS. DICKSON: Good for you. But there are many a cautionary tale bred of overconfidence. When I met the late Mr. Dickson he was near sixty and I forgave his infatuation with the opiates, for he come with this rooming house and look how many good years it's given me. Sure I cussed that damn pipe, and I cussed him for making me a widow, but sometimes we get to a point where we can't be so particular.

ESTHER *(Snaps)*: Well, I ain't going down there to be paraded like some featherless bird.

(A moment.)

I'm sorry, would you kindly take this down to Corinna Mae?

MRS. DICKSON: I'll do no such thing. You can bring it down yourself. *(Starts for the door, then abruptly stops)* It tough, Esther, for a colored woman in this city. I ain't got to tell you that. You nimble with your fingers, but all Corinna Mae got be her honey-colored skin. And you good and smart and deserve all the attention in that room, but today's her day and all I ask is that you come toast her as I know she'd toast you. Put aside your feelings—and don't say nothing about Sally's piano playing, the girl trying. For God's sake, this a party not a wake!

ESTHER: Let me fix my hair.

(Mrs. Dickson suddenly remembers the letter tucked in her dress pocket and extends it to Esther.)

MRS. DICKSON: And I thought you might want this letter. It come this morning. I didn't want to forget.

ESTHER: Who'd be writing me?

MRS. DICKSON *(Reading)*: Mr. George Armstrong.

ESTHER: It ain't someone I know. Armstrong? *(Takes the letter)* There was an Armstrong that attended my church, but he dead a long time now. Will you read the letter to me?

MRS. DICKSON: I got a house full of people. You best remind me tomorrow. And I will see you downstairs—shortly. Plenty of punch left and it better than New Year's, so best hurry. I made certain everybody be leaving this party happy.

(Mrs. Dickson exits. Esther examines the letter, then places it unopened on the sewing table. Lights crossfade: Esther lingers in half light; lights rise on a bunk in Panama. George, a muscular, handsome African Carib-

*bean man in his thirties, rises from his cot. He wipes mud from his face
and bare arms as he reads the letter. He has a musical Barbadian accent.)*

GEORGE:

Dear Miss Mills,
    My name is George Armstrong. I work in Panama along-
side Carson Wynn, your deacon's son. We digging a big hole
across the land. They say one day ships will pass from one
ocean to the next. It is important work, we told. If importance be measured by how many men die, then this be real
important work. One man drops for every twenty feet of
canal dug, like so many flies. Carson say if we eat a can of sar-
dines, they'll protect us against the mosquitoes and fever.
I say, not as long as we be digging. Lord knows our minds
deserve a bit of shade. But ain't such a thing to be had, not
here at least. Don't think me too forward, but I thought it
would be nice to have someone to think about, someone not
covered from head to toe in mud, someone to ward off this
awful boredom. Carson speaks so highly of his church that
I find comfort in his recollections. I ask if I may write you?
And if you so please, I'd welcome your words.

Sincerely,
George Armstrong

SCENE 2

*Gardenia Ball Corset: Pink Silk and
Crêpe de Chine*

*An elegant boudoir. The silhouette of a naked woman moves gracefully behind
a translucent screen. She slides her torso into fitted lingerie. Esther sits at the
dressing table exploring the carefully arranged silver grooming set. She jumps to
attention at the sound of Mrs. Van Buren's voice, which betrays the slightest
hint of a southern accent.*

MRS. VAN BUREN: I feel exposed. I think the straps need to be tightened, Esther.

ESTHER: No, ma'am, that's the way it's meant to be, but I'll add a little more fabric to—

MRS. VAN BUREN: No, no, if this is what you made for that singer, it is what I want. All right. I'm coming out.

(Mrs. Van Buren emerges from behind the dressing screen, wearing a very low corset embossed with lavender flowers. She's an attractive white woman in her early thirties, and attempts to carry herself with great poise and confidence.)

Oh God, I look ridiculous, and I'm behaving absolutely foolishly, but I'm not sure what else to do. Look at me. I've spent a fortune on feathers and every manner of accouterment. *(Esther begins to tighten the lacing of the corset)* They've written positively splendid things about me in the columns this season.

ESTHER: I'm sure they did.

MRS. VAN BUREN: But does it matter? Has he spent an evening at home? Or even noticed that I've painted the damn boudoir vermilion red?

ESTHER: You look lovely, Mrs. Van Buren.

MRS. VAN BUREN: Ha! I feel like a tart from the Tenderloin. Granted I've never been, but I'm told. Are you sure this is what you made for that . . . singer?

ESTHER: It is identical to the stitching.

(Mrs. Van Buren examines herself in the mirror, with an initial disgust that gradually gives way to curiosity.)

MRS. VAN BUREN: And you say the French women are wearing these?

ESTHER: So I'm told.

MRS. VAN BUREN: I don't believe it. It hardly seems decent. But I suppose the French aren't known for their modesty. *(Strikes a provocative, though slightly self-conscious pose)*

ESTHER: Well, it the rage. Some ladies ain't even wearing corsets in private.

MRS. VAN BUREN: Is that true?

ESTHER: Most gals don't like 'em, even fine ladies like yourself. Truth is, I ain't known a man to court pain for a woman's glance.

MRS. VAN BUREN: You're not one of those suffragettes, are you?

ESTHER: Oh God no, Mrs. Van Buren.

MRS. VAN BUREN: Indeed. I'd just as soon not tamper in men's business. *(She pours a snifter of brandy)*

ESTHER: Talk and a nickel will buy you five cents worth of trouble.

(Mrs. Van Buren gulps back the brandy.)

MRS. VAN BUREN: It's come to this. If Mother Dear could see what has become of her peach in the big city.

(Mrs. Van Buren clumsily tugs at the bodice. Esther runs her fingers gracefully along the seam, down the curve of Mrs. Van Buren's waist. Mrs. Van Buren tenses slightly at the sensation of being touched.)

(Distracted; touching the beading along the corset) Do we really need all of these dangling things?

ESTHER: Oh, I hope you ain't mind, I added a touch of beading along the trim.

MRS. VAN BUREN: It is different.

ESTHER: Do you like it?

MRS. VAN BUREN: I confess, I almost do. It's a bit naughty. *(Giggles)* Yes, I might even wear it beneath my gown tonight. Do you think anyone will notice? It is the annual Gardenia Ball, quite the event of the season.

ESTHER: So I hear.

MRS. VAN BUREN: And do you know what that means? *(A moment)* They'll all be there, parading their good fortune. I'll have to smile, be polite, because I'm known for that, but I will dread every last minute, every bit of forced conversation with the Livingstons and the Babcocks. They want to know. All of them do. "When are you going to have a child, Evangeline?" And my answer is always the same, "Why we're working on it, dear, speak to Harold." And dear Harry will be in a sour mood for a week.

You probably don't even know what I'm talking about. Have you children?

ESTHER: No, Mrs. Van Buren. I ain't been married.

MRS. VAN BUREN: Never? May I tell you something?

ESTHER: Yes. If you like.

MRS. VAN BUREN: I've given him no children. *(Whispers)* I'm afraid I can't. It's not for the lack of trying. One takes these things for granted. You assume when it comes time, that it will happen. And when it doesn't, who is to blame? They think it's vanity that's kept me childless—I've heard the women whispering. If only I were that vain. But it's like he's given up.

ESTHER: But, you're so beautiful.

MRS. VAN BUREN: You think so?

ESTHER: Yes. I can't imagine he'd ever lose interest.

MRS. VAN BUREN: But he has turned to other interests. Trust me. This will stay between us? I'm told you're discreet.

ESTHER: I just sew, missus. I don't hear anything that I ain't supposed to.

MRS. VAN BUREN: You understand why. I'd rather not be a divorcée—at my age it would prove disastrous.

ESTHER: Do you think there's something wrong with a woman alone?

MRS. VAN BUREN: What I think is of little consequence. If I were *(Whispers)* brave, I'd collect my things right now and find a small clean room some place on the other side of the park—no, further, in fact. And I'd . . . But it isn't a possibility, is it?

(A moment.)

ESTHER *(Suddenly)*: I don't know that I'll marry.

MRS. VAN BUREN: Of course you will. It's just a matter of finding the right gentleman.

ESTHER: Ma'am, I don't want to speak out of turn. But, I been working since I was nine years old with barely a day's rest. In fact, the other evening I was at my sewing machine and I stopped work and all this time had passed, gone. Years really. And I known right there that some things ain't meant to be. And that's all right, ain't it? And I wouldn't have thought no more about it, but then I got this— *(Stops mid-thought; busies herself with her sewing basket)*

MRS. VAN BUREN: Yes?

ESTHER: I'm almost ashamed to say it. At my age it foolish, I know.

MRS. VAN BUREN: What is it?

ESTHER: A gentleman . . . A gentleman has taken interest in me.

MRS. VAN BUREN: Really? How wonderful! Is he respectable?

ESTHER: I don't know. I mean, I don't know him actually. I got me this letter from Panama. A man in Panama. He wrote about two weeks back. I been carrying it around since. But, I ain't so sure I should answer.

MRS. VAN BUREN: And why not?

ESTHER: I ain't much of a writer.

MRS. VAN BUREN: Oh—

ESTHER: No, I ain't a writer at all. The fact is I can't read.

MRS. VAN BUREN: Do you have the letter? May I see it?

(Esther hesitates, then pulls the letter from her smock and hands it to Mrs. Van Buren, who quickly peruses it. She smiles.)

Panama. He has lovely penmanship—that's important. He isn't careless with his stroke—that's the mark of a thoughtful man. It's a good thing, I believe.

ESTHER: I won't respond, of course, if it ain't appropriate.

MRS. VAN BUREN: Nonsense. He's halfway across the world. I'm sure he's perfectly harmless. A bit lonesome perhaps, that's all.

ESTHER: But, if I have Mrs. Dickson over at the rooming house help me, she'll get all up in my business. And she's got an opinion about everything, and I'd rather not be lectured or questioned or bothered. She's just about the busiest . . . In any event, she said to rip it up promptly, a decent woman wouldn't resort to such a dalliance. But as you can see he has taken interest in me.

MRS. VAN BUREN: Would you like me to help you write to him, Esther?

ESTHER: I couldn't ask.

MRS. VAN BUREN: You needn't, I insist.

ESTHER: I never done this before.

MRS. VAN BUREN: Nor have I.

ESTHER: Maybe it ain't such a good idea, Mrs. Van Buren. I ain't really got much to say.

MRS. VAN BUREN: Goodness, of course you do—

ESTHER *(With conviction)*: No, I don't! I live in a rooming house with seven unattached women and sew intimate apparel for ladies, but that ain't for a gentleman's eyes. Sure I can tell him anything there is to know about fabric, but that hardly seems a life worthy of words.

MRS. VAN BUREN: It is a beginning. Come Esther, don't be shy.

(Mrs. Van Buren sits at her dressing table and retrieves a sheet of stationery.)

Now, how shall we start?

ESTHER: I don't know.

MRS. VAN BUREN: What sort of things do you like to do?

ESTHER: I . . . I go to church every Sunday, well practically, but I don't really listen to the sermons, I just like the company and the singing of course . . . And on Tuesdays . . . I take the trolley downtown to Orchard Street, and I climb five flights, in darkness, to this tiny apartment. And, when I open the door my eyes are met . . .

(Lights rise on Mr. Marks, a handsome Orthodox Jewish man in his thirties, entering with a bolt of gorgeous flowing fabric, which he proudly displays. Lost in the sweet recollection, Esther resumes speaking:)

He keeps a wealth of fabric in that apartment. He got everything you need, even things you don't know you need—

MRS. VAN BUREN: Esther, you're jumping a bit ahead of yourself.

(Lights fade on Mr. Marks.)

Shall we begin with "Dear Mr. Armstrong—"

ESTHER: Yes. That's good. "Dear Mr. Armstrong—"

MRS. VAN BUREN: "I received your letter . . ."

(Lights crossfade. George enters in his work clothes. The crossfade should allow time for Esther and George to dwell on the stage together for a few moments.)

GEORGE:

Dear Miss Mills,

I received your letter. It two months in the coming, so please forgive me, I've already written you twice since. I am most happy to make your acquaintance, and I'm anxious to hear all about you. As for me, I'd like to report on our good progress, but it isn't the case. This canal seem a near impossible mission, but here we be, digging until day end, bathed in mud up to our necks. They say a mad Frenchman dreamed up this Panama project and convinced the devil to give him an army of workers. The price—this great fissure across the land that reach right into the earth's belly. Indeed, chaos is a jackhammer away—that's what be said here anyway. But when the great oceans meet and the gentlemen celebrate, will we colored men be given glasses to raise? Today we severed the roots of a giant flamboyant, and watched it tumble to the ground. I stood thigh deep in crimson blossoms, swathed in the sweet aroma of death and wondered how a place so beautiful could become a morgue. But the days aren't all bad. If you take a moment to listen to the forest around us, there is so much life just out of sight. And there be men from every corner of the Caribbean, sharing tales around fires, heads light on rum and laughter. But now I read your letter. I see you sitting at your sewing machine. I hear the sound of the wheel turning, the tiny stitches drawing together the pieces of satin. They got machines here that take six men to operate, and slice through stone like butter. All this wonder and waste, but your letter be the most splendid thing and shall ride in me pocket, until the next.

Yours considerately,
George Armstrong

SCENE 3

Imperial Silk: Embroidered with Blue Thread

Another bedroom in a cramped tenement flat. It is small and cluttered with bolts of fabric. Mr. Marks scrambles to put on his suit jacket as a knock sounds on the door. His worn black suit is missing the top button. He hastily folds up his bedroll and opens the door, breathless. Esther stands in the doorway. She notices the bedroll but chooses to ignore it.

ESTHER: Mr. Marks? Am I too early?

MARKS: No, not at all. Come in. Come in. I've a number of new things to show you.

ESTHER: Good—

MARKS: Ah. Let me get . . . *(Unrolling an extraordinary length of silk)* Feel this one. Japanese silk, your special order for the lady on Fifth Avenue. It took me nearly one month to find this very piece. I had to go everywhere. Lovely, yes?

ESTHER *(Feeling the silk)*: Lovely. Look at how finely embroidered. Beautiful. I never—

MARKS: I have two extra yards left. I give to you for next to nothing, if you'd like.

ESTHER: Next to nothing is too much for me. You know my answer. What will I do with it?

MARKS: Make something lovely for yourself.

ESTHER: It will be wasted on me.

MARKS: You'll never see this again. I guarantee. I'll let our Fifth Avenue lady cover the difference. How about that? I see how much you like. I promise it is the very best quality. She don't know what she has—she don't come down here to feel the fabric herself, to feel the difference, the texture—she don't know how remarkable a weave.

ESTHER: I could make a shawl.

MARKS *(Fishing)*: Or a smoking jacket for your gentleman, perhaps.

ESTHER *(Bashfully)*: My gentleman? Oh no. *(Self-consciously runs the fabric across her face, then releases it)* You've distracted me, Mr. Marks. You always get me to buy something I don't need.

MARKS: When I see something of quality, I like to share with my favorite customers. Everybody want the same thing. But you want different. I like that.

ESTHER: Thank you.

(Mr. Marks smiles warmly at Esther. She averts her eyes, allowing them to fall on the spot where he's missing a button. He self-consciously touches the spot.)

MARKS: Ah, look at that. I have lost a button. *(Returning his attention to the silk)* I buy at the docks yesterday morning—it come right off a ship from the Orient. I see it and think Esther Mills will like. Of course. Everybody else: gabardine, wool, nainsook. *(Flirtatiously)* But it isn't often that something so fine and delicate enters the store. Look at the way the gold thread is interwoven; a hand took the time to gently wind it through each and every stitch like a magician. It is magnificent, yes? You'll make something exquisite. I can see from your hands that you are blessed with the needle and the thread, which means you'll never be without warmth.

ESTHER: I'm afraid it was either learn to sew or turn back sheets for fifty cents a day.

MARKS: You make it sound too simple. My father sew, my brother sew, yes, for the finest families. But I don't have the discipline, the fingers. Look at the size of these hands. Like Cirnati, Romanian sausage. I wish for your hands.

(Esther laughs and returns to examining the fabric, reveling in the tactile pleasure of its texture. There is a sensual quality to how Esther regards the fabric. Mr. Marks can't help but notice this. She brings the fabric to her nose and sniffs. Marks watches her with genuine delight.)

ESTHER: It's fruit dye. Am I right? It smells like—

MARKS: —an imperial palace; it is signed by the artist right there. I wouldn't be surprised if it was created for an empress.

ESTHER: You really want me to buy this, don't you? All right, it means I'll go without sugar for a week, will that make you happy?

MARKS: It makes you happy, it makes me happy.

ESTHER: Oh Lord, I do want it.

(Esther affectionately grasps Mr. Marks's hand; he abruptly pulls it away. Esther is taken aback.)

The color won't rub off on you.

MARKS: No, no. I'm sorry. It's not that. Please. My religious belief doesn't permit me to touch a woman who isn't my wife or my relative.

ESTHER: Oh, I see.

MARKS: It is the rabbinical law, not mine.

ESTHER: Your wife must be a happy woman.

MARKS: I am not married. Not yet. My fiancée is in Romania. Um . . . my family made the arrangement years ago.

ESTHER: Oh? I bet you miss her something awful.

(Marks rubs his hand where Esther touched him. He laughs, a bit self-consciously.)

MARKS: I haven't ever met her, actually.

(Lights crossfade to:)

SCENE 4

Heliotrope Handkerchief

Mayme's boudoir. A canopy bed dominates. Mayme, a strikingly beautiful thirty-year-old African American woman, sits at an upright piano. She plays a frenzied, upbeat rag. Her silk robe is torn and her face trembles with outrage. Esther bangs on the door. Mayme stops playing the piano and answers the door. Esther enters carrying a carpetbag.

ESTHER: I been knocking for ages. Didn't you hear me? . . . What's going on?

(A moment.)

MAYME: They really do make me sick. Always stinking of booze. And look what he done. It's the only pretty thing I own and look what he done. *(Mayme pulls the torn silk robe tight around her body)*
ESTHER: That ain't nothing; I can fix it for you.
MAYME: All the pawing and pulling. For a dollar they think they own you.

(Mayme quickly washes her face and privates in a basin.)

You don't approve of me, Esther, I don't mind. Sit. I'm awfully glad to see ya, 'am. When you knocked on the door I thought, Christ Almighty, not another one. I'm so damn tired, I don't know what to do.

(Mayme sits down at the upright piano and gracefully plays a slow, well-considered rag.)

ESTHER: Oh, pretty. Did you write that, Mayme?
MAYME: Yeah . . . *(Continuing to play)* My daddy gave me twelve lashes with a switch for playing this piece in our parlor. One for each year I studied the piano. He was too proper to like anything colored, and a syncopated beat was about the worst crime you could commit in his household. *(Stops playing)* I woke up with the sudden urge to play it.
ESTHER: You must have gotten a lot of licks in your time.
MAYME: Yeah, baby, I wasn't born this black-and-blue.

(Mayme picks up a bottle of moonshine and takes a belt.)

ESTHER: That there the reason you tired; that ignorant oil is unforgiving. Best let it lie.
MAYME: Oh bother, stop playing mother hen and come show me what you got.
ESTHER: Anything else, mistress?
MAYME: Hush your mouth, you're far too sweet for sarcasm.

(Esther pulls a corset from her bag. It's pale blue with lines of royal blue glass beads ornamenting the bodice, like Mrs. Van Buren's.)

(Touched) Is that for me?

(Mayme leaps up from the piano and holds the corset up to her body.)

ESTHER: I made one just like it for a lady on Fifth Avenue.
MAYME: It's so pretty. This is really for me? No kidding? Can I try it on?
ESTHER: Of course you can.
MAYME: Feel it. It feels like Fifth Avenue, does. You outdone yourself this time, honey.
ESTHER: Stop talking and put it on. *(Mayme gives Esther a kiss on the cheek)* And look at the flowers, ain't they sweet? It took me a whole day just to sew them on.

(Mayme takes off her robe and puts on the corset over her camisole.)

MAYME: For shame. This the prettiest thing anybody ever made for me. Truly.
ESTHER: You know that white lady I talk about sometime—hold on—

(Mayme grabs the bedpost, as Esther pulls the corset tight.)

She keep asking me what they be wearing up in the Tenderloin. All that money and high breeding and she want what you wearing.
MAYME: No kidding?
ESTHER: What she got, you want; what you got, she want.
MAYME: Onliest, I ain't got the money to pay for it. *(Modeling the corset)* Whatcha think? Do I look like a Fifth Avenue bird?
ESTHER: Grand. You look grand. Mr. Marks say that satin foulard was made for the finest ladies in Paris.
MAYME: No kidding.
ESTHER: I wasn't going to buy it. But, oh Lord, if he didn't talk me into it.
MAYME: Mr. Marks? *(A moment)* Who is this Mr. Marks?
ESTHER: He just a salesman. That's all.

MAYME: It sound to me like you a bit sweet on him.

ESTHER: Me? Oh no, he a Jew.

MAYME *(Looking into Esther's eyes)*: And? I been with a Jew, with a Turk even. And let me tell ya, a gentle touch is gold in any country.

ESTHER: I see the bodice is a bit snug—

MAYME: Is he handsome?

ESTHER: I ain't noticed.

MAYME: Good, patient Esther. Come, he wouldn't be your first, would he?

ESTHER: I ain't listenin'.

MAYME *(Softening her tone)*: You dear thing.

(Mayme laughs long and hard. Esther doesn't respond.)

No kidding. I can't even remember what it was like. Ain't that something.

ESTHER: Let's not talk about this.

MAYME: Mercy, what you must think of me. *(Suddenly self-conscious, she touches the beading on the corset)*

ESTHER: And if you must know, I'm being courted by a gentleman.

MAYME: Courted by a gentleman. Beg my pardon. Not that Panama man? Oh come on, don't tell me you still writing him.

ESTHER: He writing me.

MAYME: You'd rather a man all the way across the ocean than down Broadway? Are you expecting him to arrive in the mail like some tonic from a catalog?

ESTHER: Please don't make sport, Mayme.

MAYME: I'm just playing with you.

ESTHER *(Wounded)*: I ain't expectin' nothing.

(A moment. Mayme acknowledges Esther's hurt. She caresses her friend's face.)

MAYME: Sure you are. Sure you are, honey. Who ain't? *(Sits on the bed, beside Esther)* I am a concert pianist playing recitals for audiences in Prague and I have my own means, not bad for a colored girl from Memphis . . .

(Mayme goes to the piano and plays a few bars of classical music, per-haps allowing it to become a rag.)

And Madame always takes tea twice a week with her dear friend, Miss Esther Mills, who's known in circles for . . . for what? I forget.

(Esther is reluctant to share her dream.)

Come on, Miss Esther, don't be proud.

ESTHER: I own a quaint beauty parlor for colored ladies.

MAYME: Of course.

ESTHER: The smart set. Some place east of Amsterdam, fancy, where you get pampered and treated real nice. 'Cause no one does it for us. We just as soon wash our heads in a bucket and be treated like mules. But what I'm talking about is some place elegant.

MAYME: Go on, missy, you too fancy for me.

(Esther allows herself to get lost in the fantasy.)

ESTHER: When you come in Miss Mayme, I'll take your coat and ask, "Would you like a cup of tea?"

MAYME: Why, thank you.

ESTHER: And I'll open a book of illustrations, and show you the latest styles.

MAYME: I can pick anything in the book?

ESTHER: Yes.

MAYME: How about if I let you choose?

ESTHER: Very well. Make yourself comfortable; put your feet up, I know they're tired.

MAYME: Shucks, you don't know the half of it.

ESTHER: And in no time flat—for the cost a ride uptown and back— you got a whole new look.

MAYME: Just like that? I reckon I'd pay someone good money to be treated like a lady. It would be worth two, three days on my back. Yes, it would.

ESTHER: You think so?

MAYME: I know so.

ESTHER: And if I told you I got a little something saved? I keep it sewed up in the lining of a crazy quilt.

MAYME: On a cold, lonely night wouldn't that quilt be a poor woman's dream.

ESTHER: I been saving it slowly since I come North. It for that beauty parlor. I ain't told nobody that. Honest, for true.

MAYME: Where'd you get such a damn serious face?

ESTHER: Why not?

MAYME: Because, we just fooling that's all. I ain't been to Prague, ain't never gonna go to Prague.

ESTHER: But come, is this what you want to be doing ten years from now, twenty?

MAYME: You think I ain't tried to make a go of it. You think I just laid down and opened my legs 'cause it was easy. It don't look like nothing, but this saloon is better than a lot of them places—ask anybody. Only last night one of Bert Williams' musicians sat up front, and he stayed through the entire show. You think some of those gals in the big revues didn't start right where I am.

ESTHER: You got this beautiful piano that you play better than anyone I know. There are a dozen church choirs—

MAYME: Let me tell you, so many wonderful ideas been conjured in this room. They just get left right in that bed there, or on this piano bench. They are scattered all over this room. Esther, I ain't waiting for anybody to rescue me. My Panama man come and gone long time now. It sweet that he write you, but, my dear, it ain't real.

ESTHER: Yes, he here in my pocket in a cambric walking suit. He has a heliotrope handkerchief stuffed in his pocket and a sweet way about him. He so far away, I can carry him in my pocket like a feather. *(Laughs, producing a letter from her apron)*

MAYME: You're funny. You and your silly letter.

ESTHER: Ain't a week go by without one. It got so I know the postman by name. *(Holds out the letter)*

MAYME: I ain't interested. Put it away.

ESTHER: C'mon, Miss Mayme . . . don't be proud, you know you want to read it. *(Dangles the letter, threatening to put it away at any moment)*

MAYME: Hell, give it here. *(Snatches the letter and quickly peruses it, allowing herself a smile)* Ooo.

ESTHER: What it say?

MAYME: Your man got himself a new pair of socks. Wait . . . uh-oh, he askin' what you look like. Ain't you told him?

ESTHER: No. I'm afraid, I ain't known what to say.

MAYME: Tell him the truth.

ESTHER: That I don't look like much.

MAYME: You tell him that you're about as lovely a person as there is.

ESTHER: You know that ain't so.

MAYME: Of course it is. And what does it matter? You think half the men that come in here bother looking at my face. No ma'am. He don't care about this. *(Grabs Esther's face and gives her a kiss on the forehead)*

(Playfully showing off her physical attributes, which are accentuated by the formfitting lingerie) He interested in this, my dear. This is what he's asking about. *(Laughs)*

ESTHER: I wouldn't dare write about something like that. He Christian!

MAYME: And it's in his weakness that he'll find his strength. Hallelujah! C'mon, I'm just playing with you.

ESTHER: I'm being serious and you got your mind in the gutter.

MAYME: Oh for God's sake, the man just asking what you look like 'cause he want something pretty to think about come sundown.

ESTHER: You reckon? Then will you help me write something?

MAYME *(Hands back the letter to Esther)*: No, what about your white lady? Why not have her do it?

(A moment. Esther opens her carpetbag.)

ESTHER: 'Cause I'm asking you, my friend.

MAYME: No, my writing ain't perfect.

ESTHER: Don't bother about the handwriting, we'll tell him I pricked my finger while sewing. He'll understand. Please.

MAYME: Oh.

(Mayme fetches a sheet of paper and a pen and sits on the bed. Esther sits next to her.)

I ain't romantic, I find this silly, really I do. Only 'cause it's you. So, how do I begin?

ESTHER: "Dear George."

(Mayme concentrates, then slowly writes.)

MAYME *(Savoring the notion)*: A love letter to a gentleman. Yes, I know: "Dear George, I write you wearing a lavender silk robe with—"

(Esther giggles. Lights crossfade to George, who enters carrying a lantern. He is soaked through by the rain.)

GEORGE:

Dear Esther,

Thank you for your sweet words. Your pricked finger delivered the most unexpected lift. It quiet now. The only motion is the rain. The only sound is the rain. It is the white season, and the work all but stop. The rum shop be the onliest business that do prosper. I seen months of hard work lost in an evening, and good men befriend the devil overnight. And if I told you it's been months since I've seen a decent woman, it wouldn't be a lie. There are caravans of sweet-faced Indian girls offering up their childhood for a half day's wage. Yes, many men leave here with less than they come. I shan't be one. It isn't appropriate, but I will say it. I crave a gentlewoman's touch, even if it only be to turn down my collar or brush away the dirt in the evenings. Indeed, I'd like to meet you as a gentleman. I think much about the suit I will wear, and the colors that your eyes find pleasing. I imagine your cobblestone roads and the splendid carriages on the avenues, and a dry place to sit. I think of you running silk thread between your fingers and find a bit of holy relief, for your letters arrive just in time to ward off temptation.

Yours affectionately,
George

(Lights crossfade to:)

SCENE 5

Hand-Dyed Silk

Esther's bedroom. Esther sits at the sewing machine working on a silk camisole.
Mrs. Dickson enters carrying a letter, which she hands to Esther.

MRS. DICKSON: I don't trust him, not one bit. He writes too often.

ESTHER: It's open.

MRS. DICKSON: I'm sorry, I opened it by mistake. I didn't mean to, but
I'm glad I did.

ESTHER: 'Cause you the landlady don't give you the right to tamper
with my things.

MRS. DICKSON: What are your intentions?

ESTHER: We corresponding. That's all.

MRS. DICKSON: I know these kind of men. Sugared words, but let
them stick to the page and go no further. He'll steal your common sense, he will, and walk away. It just don't seem like you,
Esther, you're too practical a girl for this.

ESTHER: Don't set your clock by my habits.

MRS. DICKSON: His tone is very familiar. And I don't approve.

ESTHER: I'm sorry, but I needn't your approval.

MRS. DICKSON: My goodness. I hope you ain't expecting anything to
come of this.

ESTHER: And if I am?

MRS. DICKSON: Our Mr. Charles has asked me twice about you this
week. I told him he was most welcome to call.

ESTHER: Mr. Charles is a fool and a glutton. And I'm sure he don't
even know who I am.

MRS. DICKSON: You are a stubborn little country girl. And very particular. And it wouldn't hurt you to be more receptive.

ESTHER: To who? Mr. Charles? Remember it's me you're talking to,
not Doreen or Erma, or one of those other silly openhearted little gals. And yes, I'm writing letters to a man. And it may come
to nothing. But I am his sweetheart twice a month, and I can fill
that envelope with anything that I want.

MRS. DICKSON: Yes. It's an innocent enough flirtation, and I had my share in my youth. And believe me when I say I was romanced by many bright and willing young men. *(Taking Esther's hand)* It's potent, I know, but I ain't ashamed to admit that my pride ultimately led to compromise. And if you're not careful, Esther—

ESTHER: DON'T! This quilt is filled with my hard work, one hundred dollars for every year I been seated at that sewing machine. It's my beauty parlor. So you see I don't need Mr. Charles for his good job and position.

MRS. DICKSON *(Pulling the quilt off the bed)*: You think this is enough? Do you? You think this gonna make you happy when another half dozen girls waltz away in camisoles of your making. When the Bellman's Ball come around another year and you here fluffing ruffles for some girl from Kentucky, who just happy to be wearing shoes.

ESTHER: No, I don't think that. And I'd give this quilt and everything in it to be with someone I care for, I would.

MRS. DICKSON: This man in Panama—he's paper—and I'll show how easily he goes away. *(Rips up the letter.)*

ESTHER: Mrs. Dickson!

MRS. DICKSON: You'll thank me.

(Mrs. Dickson exits.
Esther picks up the pieces of the letter. Lights crossfade to George in Panama as he picks up pieces of fabric.)

GEORGE:

Dear Esther,

I opened the letter and these tiny bits of fabric tumbled out onto the ground. Imagine my surprise: gray wool, pink silk and the blue flannel, which I tucked in the back of my shirt this morning—

(Lights crossfade to Mr. Marks's bedroom. Esther touches the various fabrics: —muslin, taffeta, satin, tulle. Mr. Marks unfurls a cobalt blue roll of silk, then a vibrant roll of magenta silk.)

MARKS: It is hand-dyed silk, I washed it yesterday, and look. *(Holds up the magenta cloth)*

ESTHER *(Focused on the cobalt silk)*: Yes, beautiful.

MARKS *(Noticing Esther's attention)*: Have you ever seen anything like that?

ESTHER: No.

MARKS: It looks fragile, but feel.

(Esther runs her hand across the blue material and smiles.)

Ah, it will feel even better against your back.

ESTHER: The ladies will like this indeed. You shouldn't have shown me this . . .

(She pulls the blue fabric around her shoulders. He then wraps a strip of the magenta cloth around his shoulders.)

MARKS: Look at this color.

ESTHER: It look very good on you, Mr. Marks.

MARKS: Does it?

(Esther laughs, then Mr. Marks laughs. An awkward moment, fraught with the unspoken attraction that lies between them.)

ESTHER: Your button?

MARKS: I forget.

ESTHER: If you take off your jacket, I'll sew it on for you.

MARKS: Don't worry. It is fine. *(Buttons the remaining buttons on the coat)*

ESTHER: It'll take me no time.

MARKS: No. Thank you. Truly. It is fine.

(A moment.)

ESTHER: Why do you always wear black? You sell all of these magnificent colors, and yet every time I see you, you're wearing black.

MARKS: You ask a very complicated question. It's an act of faith—that is the simplest way I know how to explain. It is one of the many ways that I show my devotion to God.

(A moment.)

ESTHER: Is marrying someone you don't know another?

MARKS: It is a thousand years of history and struggle behind the answer to that question.

ESTHER: And yet it seems as simple as taking off a jacket. *(A moment)* I'm sorry, I didn't mean to upset you.

MARKS: You haven't upset me.

ESTHER: If you wrap the magenta, I'll pay you next week.

MARKS: To answer your question, it has always been that way in my family.

ESTHER: But this a new country.

MARKS: But we come with our pockets stuffed, yes. We don't throw away nothing for fear we might need it later . . . I wear my father's suit. It is old, I know, but this simple black fabric is my most favorite. Why? Because when I wear it, it reminds me that I live every day with a relationship to my ancestors and God.

(As Mr. Marks turns to wrap the fabric, Esther ever so gently touches the back of his collar. He doesn't register the gesture. Or does he?

Lights crossfade to Mrs. Van Buren's boudoir. Mrs. Van Buren wears a lacy kimono and corset made of hand-dyed magenta silk.)

MRS. VAN BUREN: Hand-dyed silk? Is it popular?

ESTHER: It will be by fall.

MRS. VAN BUREN: Really? I'll have to weave that tidbit into conversation this evening. My in-laws are coming. The frog and the wart. Oh, and did I tell you? I saw Mr. Max Fiedler of Germany conduct selections from *Don Juan*. I had to endure an encore from the soprano—what was her name? Something Russian, no doubt. I'd rather have gone to the electric show at Madison Square Garden, but you see, Harry isn't impressed with electricity: "Miracle upon miracle, but there remain things science will never be able to give us," he says, so he refrains from enthusiasm. By the way, I bled this morning, and when I delivered the news to Harry, he spat at me. This civilized creature of society. We all bleed, Esther. And yet I actually felt guilt, as though a young girl again apologizing for becoming a woman.

(Mrs. Van Buren sheds her kimono, fully revealing the low-cut magenta corset, with pale pink camisole beneath.)

Maybe I'll be a bohemian. A bohemian needn't a husband, she's not bound by convention.

ESTHER: I don't see why you let him do you this way, missus. If you don't mind me saying.

(A moment.)

MRS. VAN BUREN: Have you been to the opera?

(Aware that she overstepped, Esther nervously adjusts the bodice.)

ESTHER: Never.
MRS. VAN BUREN: Oh God, you're lucky. It's one of those things required of me. I'm certain you've found a more engaging means of entertainment.
ESTHER: I actually only been to the theatre once.
MRS. VAN BUREN: Really? What did you see?
ESTHER: Nothing special. A blind gal from Alabama sang spirituals. I need you to lift your arms.
MRS. VAN BUREN: Like this? *(Playfully, seductively, she lifts her arms)* It's pinching me right here.

(Esther ignores Mrs. Van Buren's playfulness. She stands behind Mrs. Van Buren and wraps her arms around her torso. She runs her fingers along the top of the corset, then reaches in to adjust her breast. Esther tightens the bodice as Mrs. Van Buren continues:)

I've never been to a colored show, I'm told they're quite good.
ESTHER: I suppose.
MRS. VAN BUREN: I should like to see one for myself. You must take me to one of your shows.

ESTHER: And will you take me to the opera next time you go?

MRS. VAN BUREN: I would . . . if I could. It would be marvelously scandalous, just the sort of thing to perk up this humdrum season.

(Mrs. Van Buren touches Esther's hand with an unexpected tenderness. Esther politely withdraws her fingers.)

It is so easy to be with you. *(Whispers)* Your visits are just about the only thing I look forward to these days. You, and our letters to George, of course. Shall we write something dazzling to him? Something delicious?

(A moment. Esther seems hesitant.)

ESTHER: But, if—

MRS. VAN BUREN: What? Why not?

ESTHER: Perhaps something simple this time—I believe there real affection growing.

MRS. VAN BUREN: Yes, one would hope. He seems quite taken.

ESTHER: I don't want him to be disappointed.

MRS. VAN BUREN: And he needn't be. We'll send him your warmth and he'll find you irresistible.

ESTHER: Do you think we could describe this silk? *(Runs her fingers down the front of Mrs. Van Buren's silk corset)* Will you tell him what it feel like against your skin? How it soft and supple to the touch. I ain't got the words, but I want him to know this color, magenta red. What it make you feel right now. It—

MRS. VAN BUREN: The silk? Are you sure?

ESTHER: Yes.

MRS. VAN BUREN: Mercy, if my friends knew I spend the day writing love letters to a colored laborer, they'd laugh me out of Manhattan.

ESTHER: People do a lot of things that they don't ever speak of.

MRS. VAN BUREN: I smoked opium once, with the most proper of women. She dared me and I did it. And you? What have you done?

(A moment.)

ESTHER: I touched someone . . . who I knew I wasn't supposed to touch. I touched them because I wanted to. It was wrong, but I couldn't help myself.

(Mrs. Van Buren takes in Esther's words. She exits.

The lights crossfade to George sitting on his bunk. He's illuminated by a kerosene lantern. Esther remains on stage in half light; it's as if she is listening to George speak directly to her.)

GEORGE:

Dearest Esther,

It dawn. No work has begun. The morning is still holding the ocean, not yet blue. But I can see past everything green to the horizon. And it is here in half light that I imagine you. Six months have passed since our first correspondence, and much has changed. A water boy from my parish died, taken by fever two nights past. All their magic machinery and there's nothing could be done for this boy. It got me thinking about his family behind and the wife he'd never meet. He die so easy. Why he? His young life end, and not more than a word from the Yankee chief, 'cept regret that the new boy ain't so quick. This morn I try to remember his small black-ened face and cannot even recall his smile, though his hand give me water each and every day since I be here. Why this boy go out my mind, I ask? Tomorrow I too could be sucked into the ground without tears, and ride the death train that pass through here five times a day. When I first come, a solid ox was the dream of this man. But I watch the splendid way the American gentlemen touch their fine machines and laugh away the jungle, and I know what great and terrible things their sleep brings. And yet, your America sounds like a wondrous place; a man such as myself would be willing to surrender much for a taste of the modern world. Yes, I see beyond the tilting palms, through the mangroves and across the Caribbean sea to where you sit. I kneel beside you at this moment, and I tell you: I am a good, strong man. What I've come to feel for you can best be described as love. I love you. There is no other way to say it. Will you marry me?

Most adoringly,
George

(Lights crossfade to:)

S CENE 6

White   Cotton   Bed   Linen

Mayme's boudoir. Mayme hangs a pair of wet stockings on the bedpost.

MAYME: Why ya smiling so big? Close your mouth 'fore your teeth dry out.

ESTHER: He's asked me to marry him.

MAYME: What? No kiddin'.

ESTHER: It in writin'.

MAYME: Show me. *(Esther hands Mayme the letter)* Our own Miss Esther.

ESTHER: He say he loves me.

MAYME: And do you love him?

ESTHER: As much as you can love a man you ain't seen. I'm thirty-five, Mayme, and he wants to marry me. And there ain't gonna be no more opportunities I'm afraid. I've told him yes.

MAYME: Well, goddamn. I'm sure he's a fine man.

ESTHER: Yes, I suppose. Any man go through this much trouble to court a woman must have his virtues.

MAYME: I reckon.

ESTHER: He write that he arriving next month.

MAYME: That soon . . . you hardly ready.

ESTHER: I know. I'm getting married! Oh God, will you come to witness the ceremony?

MAYME: Me? You want to bring me around your new husband?

ESTHER: It would be nice to have a friend witness.

MAYME: No. I ain't been to church since I was seventeen. It ain't about you—it's just a promise I made to myself years ago. I ain't got nothing to say to God, and it don't seem right to go up into somebody's home and you ain't on speaking terms.

ESTHER: It just a building.

MAYME: Just the same, I'd rather not be reminded. But thank you, my dear, it's a long time since I been invited anyplace proper.

ESTHER: Me, too.

(Mayme laughs and grabs a bottle of liquor.)

MAYME: Hell, we ought to celebrate. Somebody give me this gin. It look expensive. Whatcha think? Should I open it?

ESTHER: Sure. Why not.

MAYME *(Pouring them each a glass of gin)*: We gonna toast to one less spinster in New York.

ESTHER: Oh God, I hope I ain't making a mistake.

MAYME: You'll be fine. You're about the most sensible gal I know. Enjoy this, honey. It's a splendid feeling. Yes, indeed. I was engaged once. You won't tell nobody. A mortician's apprentice who hated music. Need I say more.

ESTHER: Do you regret not marrying him?

MAYME: Some days—no—some evenings, honey. *(Raising her glass into the air)* But here's to Esther: You will be a beautiful bride, and may happiness follow.

(They toast and drink. Mayme sits at the piano.)

My dear, you're gonna go to socials and other ridiculous functions that married folk attend, drink lots of lemonade, God forbid, and become an awful gossip. And you know, it won't be appropriate to visit a place like this.

ESTHER: Who say?

MAYME *(Snaps)*: I say.

(A moment.)

ESTHER: We friends. Ain't no Panama man gonna change that.

MAYME: Well, I hope he is wonderful.

(Mayme starts to play piano. Singing:)

Give me a man that'll come and bake me a cake.
Put in some sugar and spice.
Yes, he can put it in my oven any ol' time
And watch it rise on up.
Give me a man that'll come and mow my lawn
From the front to the back.

(Esther joins in.)

MAYME AND ESTHER:

Yes, he can tend my garden any ol' time
And watch it rise on up.
A woman needs a handyman to take care of her home.
A woman needs a candy man who'll fight the bees for the
comb.

(Esther stops singing. She silently contemplates her decision, uncertain.)

MAYME:

Give me a man that'll come and bake me a cake.
Load it with some sugar and spice.
Yes, he can put it in my oven any ol' time
And watch it rise on up.

(Lights crossfade to Esther's bedroom. Mrs. Dickson is packing Esther's suitcase. Esther enters.)

MRS. DICKSON: Who is going to sit next to me at the table? There is Bertha, but she has no conversation. Oh, I could move Erma down closer, but she and Bertha don't speak. It'll be an absolute mess at the dinner table without you. That's for certain. Oh, it's gonna be a shame to let this room to anybody else. It has so many of your sweet touches. Yes.

ESTHER: You wasn't always pleased with my conversation if I recall.

MRS. DICKSON: Who told you that? Well . . . they lie! *(Holds up a dress)* Oh no, not this little frumpy thing! Really Esther, my grandmother wouldn't even wear a collar like so, and she was a right proud Christian soldier. Yes.

ESTHER: Well, I like it. It's the most refined thing I own. I paid five whole dollars for it.

MRS. DICKSON: You'll scare off your gentleman, and it ain't worth five dollars of misery. You needn't be a prude. Trust me, your man'll have needs, and it's your duty to keep his member firmly at home. Yes.

ESTHER: Excuse me?

MRS. DICKSON: I shan't repeat it. But there ain't no greater disappointment than a husband without much . . . vigor. Believe me, I know. And sometime he gotta be pleasured to ensure your own satisfaction. You understand. I ain't an expert, but I do have some experience. And I'll tell you, give-and-take make for the best of partnerships. Never mind what the minister tells you about decency—what go on between a man and wife be their own business. He will test you and he will try you, but don't let him beat on you. Don't take no shit from him, understand.

ESTHER: Mrs. Dickson.

MRS. DICKSON: Excuse me for saying, but if he raises his hand once, he'll do it again. I thought we should have this conversation before you go off. I don't mean to scare you, but I know you come as an innocent, and we're friends, so I feel I can speak plainly.

ESTHER: Thank you, but I do believe I'm old enough to handle things for myself.

MRS. DICKSON: Just the same, I thought I'd say it. Now whatcha want me to do with this dress?

ESTHER: It that bad?

MRS. DICKSON: Let's just say we'll give it to Deacon Wynn and let the church ladies fight over it. Yes. *(Sits on the bed)* You really going to do this, ain't you?

ESTHER: You didn't expect me to be here for the rest of my life?

MRS. DICKSON: I guess I sort of did. I'm so used to hearing your sewing machine and foot tapping up here. Yes, I reckon I'm going to miss it.

ESTHER: Another gal will move into this room, and by supper you'll be fussing about something new.

MRS. DICKSON: You say that with such certainty. You hurt my feelings, Miss Esther Mills. *(Dabbing her eyes with a handkerchief)* Eighteen years is a long time. Yes. I don't reckon I've known anyone else that long. It'll be lonely.

ESTHER: You have plenty of suitors to keep you busy.

MRS. DICKSON: But ain't a working man amongst them.

(A moment.)

You know, you don't have to do this.

ESTHER: Yes, I do. I stay on here, I'll turn to dust one day, get swept up and released into the garden without notice. I've finally found someone. Just as you found Mr. Dickson.

MRS. DICKSON: I married him because I was thirty-seven years old, I had no profession and there wasn't a decent colored fella in New York City that would have me.

ESTHER: But you come to love each other.

MRS. DICKSON: I suppose. He give me some laughs. But you see, my mother wanted me to marry up. She was a washerwoman, and my father was the very-married minister of our mission. He couldn't even look out at her there in the church pews, but she'd sit there proudly every Sunday, determined to gain God's favor. Marry good. She didn't ever want me to be embarrassed of my fingers the way she was of hers. I'd watch her put witch hazel and hot oil on her delicate hands, but they remained raw and chapped, and she kept them hidden inside gray wool gloves. In the winter they'd bleed so bad sometimes, but she'd plunge her hands into the hot water without flinching, knead and scrub the clothing clean. Fold and press for hours and hours—the linen, the bedding, the stockings and the britches—sometimes wearing the frayed gloves so as not to leave bloodstains on her precious laundry. She wouldn't even let me help her, she didn't want my hands to show the markings of labor. I was going to marry up. Love was an entirely impractical thing for a woman in her position. "Look what love done to me," Mama used to say. "Look what love done to me."

(A moment.)

So I did what was necessary to gain favor. I allowed myself to be flattered by gentlemen. You understand? Yes, this "pretty" gal done things, unpretty things, for this marble mantel, gaslights in every room, a player piano and an indoor toilet.

ESTHER: But Mr. Dickson was a good man.

MRS. DICKSON: Bless his broken-down soul. He had fine suits and perfect diction, and was too high on opium to notice that he was married. But I would not be a washerwoman if it killed me. And I have absolutely marvelous hands to prove it. *(Laughs, displaying her hands)* But you have godly fingers and a means, and you deserve a gentleman. Why gamble it all away for a common laborer?

ESTHER: . . . Love.

MRS. DICKSON: Don't you let a man have no part of your heart without getting a piece of his.

(Lights crossfade to George.)

GEORGE:

Dear Esther,

I held in the port of Havana, Cuba, awaiting passage to New York City. A passenger come down with cholera. So here I wait, fighting patience. We sail tomorrow—

(Crossfade to Mr. Marks's bedroom, where Mr. Marks has just finished preparing a cup of tea. Esther hesitantly enters.)

MARKS: Miss Mills, where have you been? I thought I'd lost you to a competitor. *(A moment)* I keep looking out the window at Mr. Friedlander's shop; he's giving away thread with each purchase. Yesterday, stress tonic. Tomorrow, who knows? I saw this morning Mrs. Simons—Mrs. Simons my cousin's wife—go into Mr. Friedlander's. His fabric is inferior, I tell her this, but she wants the stress tonic. Then go to the pharmacy, I say.

Where have you been? I've been going crazy. I couldn't bear to lose you to Friedlander.

ESTHER: I'm sorry, I—

MARKS: No, I'm sorry. You've been busy, of course. I thought something might have happened to you.

ESTHER: Don't tell me you were worried about me.

MARKS: Well, yes. I didn't have your address, otherwise I would have inquired about your health.

ESTHER: I'm very well, thank you.

(A moment. Esther smiles. Mr. Marks shyly looks away.)

MARKS: I found something I think you'll love. *(Excited)* Do you have a moment?

ESTHER: Yes.

MARKS: I'll get it.

(He fingers through the bolts of fabric, but suddenly stops himself. He struggles for a moment with whether to broach a question.)

I just made tea. Would you have a cup of tea with me?

ESTHER: Thank you, that would be nice.

(Mr. Marks clears a chair for Esther. She sits, now a bit disarmed by the invitation. Mr. Marks pours her a cup of tea, then one for himself. He sits down on a chair across from her. A moment. He touches the spot where the button is missing.)

MARKS: Is the tea hot enough? Milk? Would you like sugar, of course?

ESTHER: No, thank you, it's fine. *(Smiles)*

MARKS: You have a lovely smile.

(Esther stops smiling. Mr. Marks stands up, embarrassed by his candor.)

Let me show you the fabric.

ESTHER: Actually, I have a special request. I'll need fabric for a wedding gown, something simple, Mr. Marks. The bride don't got a lot of money to throw away.

MARKS: Satin? Chiffon? Cotton? Silk? Yes. Tulle?

ESTHER: Satin, I think.

MARKS: She hasn't told you?

ESTHER: Silk.

(Mr. Marks pulls down several bolts of fabric. Esther examines each one, her excitement muted.)

MARKS: That one you're touching is very popular. And the price will please you. Thirty cents a yard.

ESTHER: Twenty?

MARKS: Twenty-five cents. The bride will like.

ESTHER: It's too much. Something less expensive—I'll dress it up with lace and ribbons. *(Points to a faded old roll)* How about this one?

MARKS: It's a wedding. This is for an older woman—

ESTHER: I ain't so young.

MARKS: —the bride's mother perhaps.

(A moment.)

You are getting married?

(A moment.)

ESTHER: Yes. You seem surprised.

MARKS *(He is)*: No, no. Not at all. My congratulations.

(Mr. Marks pulls out his finest wedding fabric.)

Please. I'm sure the rich lady who ordered this didn't appreciate the delicacy of the fabric. She gave no thought to who crafted this perfection, the labor that went into making it, how many hands touched it. Look. Beautiful. You deserve to wear it on your wedding day.

ESTHER: It's so beautiful, it looks like little fairy hands made it. It's too fine for me.

MARKS: Come, touch it and then refuse. Please. Touch.

(Mr. Marks watches Esther run her fingers across the fabric. He also touches it, sensually. She closes her eyes. He continues to watch her, savoring the moment.)

It is exquisite. Miss Mills, many fine ladies have worn it against their skin, but it was made for you. I know this . . .

(Esther holds the fabric to her face and begins to weep.)

. . . May it be your first gift.

(Mr. Marks wants to offer her comfort, but he cannot touch her.)

ESTHER: I won't let you.
MARKS: It would be my pleasure.

(Esther accepts the length of fabric. They gaze at each other, neither able to articulate the depth of their feelings.

A moment.

Esther and Marks exit, as the lights rise on Mayme seated at her piano. She plays a rag.

Lights rise on Mrs. Van Buren, who enters her boudoir smoking a cigarette and nursing a glass of brandy. She studies her image in the vanity mirror.

Then we see Mr. Marks reenter his bedroom, fiddling with the buttons on his jacket. He takes out a needle and thread and contemplates whether to sew on a new button.

Lights on Mrs. Dickson, who enters carrying a wedding veil. She toys with the delicate fabric.

Then George enters in an ill-fitted, frayed gray suit—his best. He moves downstage with the uncertainty of a new arrival. Esther, dressed in a spectacular, white wedding gown, nervously enters. Mrs. Dickson places the veil on Esther's head.

Everyone but George and Esther exit. Esther joins George downstage, each of them in a separate pool of light. George and Esther look at each other, for the first time, then look out into the world. There is a flash—as from an old-fashioned flash camera. The sepia-toned image is captured. A projected title card appears above their heads: "Unidentified Negro Couple, ca. 1905."

Blackout.)

 Act Two

The Wedding Corset: White Satin Embroidered with Orange Blossoms

Esther stands in a pool of light. She wears her wedding gown. Another pool of light engulfs George. He wears his worn, gray wedding suit. Lights rise. A spare studio flat. An iron bed dominates the room, and George and Esther are standing on either side of the bed, which is covered with the crazy quilt. A silence divides them.

    Finally, Esther speaks:

ESTHER: Don't really feel much different. I guess I expected somethin' to be different. It was a nice ceremony. Didn't you think? I wish my family could a witnessed it all. My mother in particular. When the minister said, "man and wife," I nearly fainted, I did. I been waiting to hear those words since—they nearly took my breath away. "Man and wife," and the truth is we barely know each other. I've written you near everything there is to know about me, and here we is, and I fear I ain't got no more to say.

45

GEORGE (*His accent is a touch heavier and more distinctly Barbadian than before*): We ain't need to say nothin' now. We got plenty of time for that. It late.

(*George takes off his jacket and tosses it across the bed. He loosens his top button. Esther picks up the jacket, quickly surveys the label, then neatly folds it, and places it at the bottom of the bed.*)

ESTHER: Do you wish to bathe? I'll fetch the basin.

(*George kneels on the bed and extends his hand to Esther.*)

GEORGE: Why don't yuh come sit by me. Let me see yuh.

(*Esther sinks on the bed with her back to George. He gently strokes her cheek. She trembles.*)

Are yuh afraid of me? Yuh shaking.
ESTHER: Am I? None of this be familiar.
GEORGE: Give yuh hand 'ere.

(*Esther gingerly passes her hand to George. He sits next to her, kissing each of her fingers, then places her hand on his crotch.*)

See. It ain't scary at all.

(*Esther leaves her hand resting on his crotch; uncomfortable. A moment.*)

I expected yuh to be—
ESTHER: Prettier.
GEORGE: No, I was gonna say—
ESTHER: It's okay, I lived with this face all my life, ain't no surprises. We should say what we think now and get it out of the way.
GEORGE: I suppose from yuh letters—
ESTHER: I described my character. And I think you'll find me truthful.

(*George begins to unbutton Esther's dress. She stiffens at his touch.*)

You're very handsome. More than I thought, and I must say it do make me a little uncomfortable. *(Withdraws her hand from his crotch)* And the other thing I think you must know, I ain't been with a man before. I been kissed and done some kissing, but you know what I'm saying. And it might be awkward on this first night, even if we man and wife—

GEORGE: Then we'll make it less awkward.

(George slips Esther's dress off her shoulders. She's wearing a stunning wedding corset of white satin embroidered with orange blossoms. He plants a kiss on her bare back.)

Real nice. Pretty. I like it.

(George runs his fingers across the delicate lace covering her breasts.)

ESTHER: Wait. I made something for you. *(Stands up and quickly fetches the smoking jacket)*
    Here.
GEORGE: What it?
ESTHER: It's Japanese silk. Put it on.

(George clumsily pulls the smoking jacket around his muscular body. He clearly isn't comfortable with the delicacy of the garment.)

Careful.

(George explores the jacket with his weather-worn fingers.)

It ain't too small?
GEORGE: Nah. But I afraid I soil it.

(George removes the jacket and tosses it on the bed. He pulls Esther into his arms.)

ESTHER: Not yet.
GEORGE: Yuh got somethin' in mind?

ESTHER: Couldn't we wait a bit?

GEORGE: Minister say, "man and wife."

ESTHER: Please, I'd like to know about your mother or about your birthplace, Bar-ba-dos. Something I don't know. That wasn't in the letters. Something for us, right now.

(A moment.)

GEORGE: Like what?

(Esther pulls away and picks up the smoking jacket.)

ESTHER: I come here from North Carolina at seventeen after my mother died of influenza, God bless her loving spirit. My father died two years later, he was a slave you see, and didn't take to life as a freeman. He'd lost his tongue during a nasty fight over a chicken when I was a baby, so I never heard him speak: no complaints, no praise, no gentle words, no good-bye. He was . . . silent. Broken really. I come to this city by myself, worked my way North little by little, picking berries in every state until I get here. An old woman in the rooming house teach me to sew intimate apparel, saying folks'll pay you good money for your discretion. It was just about the best gift anybody give me. It was as though God kissed my hands when I first pulled the fabric through the sewing machine and held up a finished garment. I discovered all I need in these fingers.

(A moment.)

I wanted you to know that about me.

GEORGE: My parents were chattel . . . born to children of chattel. *(Takes off his shirt)* We cut sugar cane and die, and that our tale for as long as anybody could say. Nothin' worthy of a retelling, really. I come here so the story'll be different, that I hopin'. Now if yuh don' mind, I spent many nights on a hard, wood floor, a bed be long overdue. *(Esther gives him her hand)* We married. I ain' gonna commit no crime 'ere, a man and wife don't 'ave no quarrel in the bedroom.

(George gently pulls Esther onto the bed. The lights slowly fade as Esther succumbs to his embrace.

Ragtime piano. Lights rise as Mayme and Mrs. Van Buren enter, dressed in their twin corsets. They stand over the wedding bed like two apparitions.)

MAYME: What is he like?

(George climbs out of bed. He stands in a pool of light and slowly goes through the ritual of dressing. Esther kneels on her bed wrapped in the crazy quilt.)

ESTHER: He handsome enough.
MRS. VAN BUREN: Come, what did he say when he saw you?

(Esther climbs out of bed. As they speak, if necessary, Mayme and Mrs. Van Buren may help Esther dress.)

ESTHER: He ain't say much of nothing. He just stood there for a moment regarding me with his eyes. Yellow, cotton-and-cane eyes. I didn't have no tongue.
MRS. VAN BUREN: He must be something of a romantic. He traveled halfway across the world because of some promise on a paper.
ESTHER: And he still smell of salt and ground nuts. It make me sick and it make me excited.
MRS. VAN BUREN: I was tipsy on my wedding night. I recall being in love with the notion of love, and everything took on a rosy glow. Harry was foolish and confident and I was frightened to death.
MAYME: Is he as we imagined?
ESTHER: Yes, he is sturdy enough and quite a pleasure to behold. His hands thick, stained dark from work. North Carolina field hands. But he got a melodious voice, each word a song unto itself.

(Mayme and Mrs. Van Buren reluctantly retreat into the darkness.

Esther and George finish dressing. Esther continues to speak as if to the women.)

And when he finally fell asleep I placed my head on his chest, and listened for the song of cicadas at dusk, and imagined the sweet aroma of the mango trees and the giant flamboyant with its crimson tears.

(Esther and George stand on either side of the bed, dressed.)

Scene 2

Valenciennes Lace

George and Esther's bedroom. A rag plays. George smoothes down his over-grown hair, pleased with himself. His clothing is worn, but that doesn't seem to trouble him. Esther takes in George from the corner of her eye, quickly averting her gaze when he glances at her. He smiles to himself.

ESTHER: Do you want me to fix you something?

GEORGE: I ain't really hungry, you know.

ESTHER: Where are you going? It Sunday. I promised Mrs. Dickson we'd dine with her this afternoon after the church social.

GEORGE: That woman ask too many questions for me liking.

ESTHER: That's what ladies do. She's just being attentive.

(George grabs his hat and toys with it for a moment. He ventures to speak, but stops himself. Finally:)

GEORGE: Say, Mrs. Armstrong, you got two dollars?

ESTHER: What for?

GEORGE: I need a proper hat if yuh want me to look for real work. It near three months now, and this a farmer's hat, I tol'. The rag man wouldn' even give me a penny for it.

ESTHER: Two dollars. That's a lot of money. I tol' you I'd make you a worsted suit. Right smart.

GEORGE *(Gently touching Esther's hand)*: C'mon, Mrs. Armstrong. Just two dollars.

ESTHER: But this is the last time. Hear?

(Esther reluctantly goes over to the quilt and opens the seam with her scissors. She digs in and pulls out two dollars.)

There.

GEORGE: That all you got?

ESTHER: Yes. Why do you need to go out?

GEORGE: I tell some fellas I stop off for a quick ale, be back 'fore yuh know.

ESTHER: But it Sunday. I'll put on some tea—and sit, let me mend your shirt, you can't go out with a hole in your shirt. *(Touches the hole in his shirt)* What will they say about your wife? I won't hear the end of it from Mrs. Dickson.

GEORGE: She a real madam. "Yuh working, George?" "Oh, nuh?" *(Chupses[1])* I ain' been this idle since a boy in St. Lucy. But that busylickum ain' 'ear nothing. *(Chupses again)* I got me pats on the back from white engineers, and a letter of recommendation from the Yankee crew chief heself. But 'ere, I got to watch buildings going up left and right, steel girders as thick as tamarind trees, ten, twelve stories high. Thursday last I stood all day, it cold too, waitin' for the chief, waiting to interview. Do yuh have tools, boy? Yes! Do yuh know how to operate a machine, boy? Yes. But 'e point just so to the Irishman, the German and the tall Norwegian, who's at least fifty years plus five. And I got more experience than the lot. I tell 'e so. Next time, 'e say. Next time, George. Can you believe? And when everyone gone, 'e pass me this damn note like it money. *(Takes a letter from his pocket and unfolds it)* Look.

(He hands the note to Esther. She examines it, pretending to read.)

What do you t'ink?

(He watches her ever so carefully . . .)

---

1. A gesture, much like the sucking of teeth.

ESTHER: I don't know what to say. I suppose he mean what he say.
(Anxiously places the letter on the bed)
GEORGE: But what do you t'ink? You t'ink what he say true?
ESTHER: Why wouldn't he be truthful?

(Frustrated, George takes off his shirt and tosses it to Esther. He then throws himself across the bed and lights a cigarette. Esther goes about mending George's shirt by hand.)

Did you try over at that butcher's? Like I asked. I know they could use an extra man 'cause it's always crowded in there. Especially on Friday.
GEORGE: I don' know. We'll see.
ESTHER: There are worse things you could do. And I thought maybe we could go to the church social before Mrs. Dickson's.
GEORGE: I ain' a church man, really.
ESTHER *(Stops sewing)*: You do believe, don't you? Why in letters you said—
GEORGE: I say a lot of t'ings.

(A moment. Esther returns to sewing. George feels the quilt.)

ESTHER: Please, I ain't been to a social. I sat up in Saint Martin's for years, and didn't none of them church ladies bother with me until I walked in on your arm, and suddenly they want Mrs. Armstrong over for tea.
GEORGE: Yuh and yuh monkey chaser yuh mean?
ESTHER: Oh that ain't so. Most of them folks ain't been nowhere to speak of. But they are fine people, and who knows where help will come from?
GEORGE: I want to build t'ings, not polish silver or port luggage. Them fine jobs for yuh Yankee gentlemen, but not me. I ain' come 'ere for that! They'll have me a bootblack 'fore long. Let the damn Italians blacken their hands, I say. Mine been black long enough. A man at the saloon, smart-looking fella, say the onliest way for a colored man in this country is for 'e to be 'e own man. Have 'e own business, otherwise 'e always be shining

the white man nickel. You understand, no? And really, how it look to people. Me, sitting 'ere, waitin' on fortune, you out there courtin' it.

ESTHER: I am your wife, and whatever I got, yours. And George, mind your smoking on the bed. The Chinaman two floors down burn up that way.

(George puts out the cigarette.)

GEORGE: Listen, this fella at the saloon talk about a man sellin' a stable with a dozen strong draft horses. 'E in a bit of debt, and need money quick quick. A dozen horses for nothin'. Did you 'ear what I say?

(Esther stops sewing.)

ESTHER: That saloon talk. That man'll take your money to Shanghai. It just a dream—it ain't gonna feed you today.

GEORGE: You t'ink I stupid?

ESTHER: No. But supposin' he honest, where would you get the money for twelve horses?

GEORGE: Where, Mrs. Armstrong? *(Gently strokes the quilt)* Am I wrong?

ESTHER: My quilt? Never mind with that money. It just there and it gonna stay there.

GEORGE: Yuh a squirrel, for true. That's what yuh call them city rats, no?

ESTHER: A squirrel ain't a rat. That money for my beauty parlor, I told you that.

GEORGE *(Laughs)*: That funny.

ESTHER: Why's that funny to you?

GEORGE: You ownin' a beauty parlor.

ESTHER: Yes.

(George studies Esther. She self-consciously returns to sewing.)

GEORGE: Look at yuh. How yuh know pretty from the lookin' glass?

(A moment.)

ESTHER *(Wounded)*: I make pretty things.

(George pops up off the bed and takes Esther in his arms.)

GEORGE: I sorry, Mrs. Armstrong. I ain' know what I say. Yuh be real sweet, if you done up yuh hair nice. Put a little paint on yuh lips.

(George runs his hand across Esther's mouth. He grabs her and tries to do a quick dance.)

ESTHER: I ain't that kind of woman.
GEORGE: No, yuh ain'. *(Lets go of Esther's arm. Gently)* Please, Esther.
ESTHER: No. That eighteen years there.
GEORGE *(Chupses)*: Yuh vex me so. Where's me shirt?
ESTHER: It ain't finished.

(George grabs the shirt and puts it on.)

Be careful, you'll tear—
GEORGE: I going o'er to the Empty Cup for an ale. I see yuh later.
ESTHER: That a notorious place.
GEORGE: How yuh know?
ESTHER: I know.

(George chupses.)

Why are you so cross with me? You got your ale money and enough for God knows what else. Ain't that so?
GEORGE: Yes, it yuh nickel. How do t'ink that make me feel?
ESTHER: I come here with nothing.
GEORGE: Don't look at me so.
ESTHER: I slept in a cold church for nine days, and picked up bread-crumbs thrown to pigeons.
GEORGE: Yes. Yuh done good, but five hundred days digging don' amount to nothing 'ere. It always gray. Why it so gray? Work on the isthmus, it hard, but at least the sun shine.

ESTHER: I know you here 'cause of me, and I want you to be happy. We stood in that church, and promised before God to take care of each other. That means something, even if it gray. You listenin'?

GEORGE: I listenin'.

ESTHER: You got a good arm George Armstrong, and I'd be proud to walk in on it whether it shining shoes or picking cotton.

GEORGE: I just tired of comin' home to put me hand in yuh pocket.

(George grabs his hat and coat. Esther attempts to turn down his collar. He brushes her hand away.)

I off.

ESTHER: What about Mrs. Dickson and the social?

GEORGE: I be back for supper.

(George exits. Esther picks up George's work letter and crumples it up. Crossfade to Mr. Marks's bedroom. Mr. Marks hums a rag as he searches through piles of fabric. Esther enters.)

MARKS: Here it is. Scottish wool, it isn't as expensive as one would think. It is very good.

ESTHER: Are you humming a rag, Mr. Marks?

MARKS: No, it's a Romanian song. I can't remember the words. It is driving me mad.

ESTHER *(Smiles)*: I'm very happy to see that you replaced the button on your suit.

MARKS *(Proudly)*: You noticed. It was time, don't you think? *(Displaying the fabric)* You wanted Scottish wool, yes?

ESTHER: Scottish wool. Yes. *(Feeling the fabric)* It's so heavy. Would you wear a suit made of this?

MARKS: Well, yes. You see how soft it is. I bought it from a gentlemen who said it came from his village. He had a wonderful story about his mother caring for the sheep like small children. He said every night she'd tell them a fairy tale, and each morning give the creatures a kiss and a sprinkle of salt. The neighbors would watch and laugh, watch and laugh. But come time to shear the animals, what wonderful wool they produced for his mother. Like no other.

(Esther lovingly feels the fabric. Mr. Marks revels in her delight.)

He could have been a thief for all I know, but the color is a lovely coffee, very subtle. Don't you think? So I pay too much, but not enough for the quality. Ah! Yes. I have something else to show you. It's here. Where is it? Where are you? Here we are. *(Unfurls a roll of Valenciennes lace)* I almost let it go last week, but I was waiting for you. I wanted you to see it.

ESTHER *(Smiling)*: Oh, yes.

MARKS: I knew you'd like it. *(Elated)* The wait was worth seeing your smile again.

(Mr. Marks playfully drapes the lace around Esther's neck. They find themselves standing dangerously close to each other. They are so close that they can inhale each other's words. A moment.)

Miss Mills, if I may say—

ESTHER: Armstrong. *(Removes the lace from her shoulders)*

MARKS: I apologize. I forget. I forget.

(A moment. Mr. Marks takes the lace and places it on the cutting board.)

ESTHER: It is pretty, thank you. But today I've come for fabric for a gentleman's suit. Next time.

MARKS: Yes. Just a minute, I have some other wools, gabardine, if you'd like to see. I have no story for them, but they are sturdy and reliable, will give you no problems.

(As Mr. Marks turns to search for another bolt of fabric, Esther gently runs her fingers across the lace. Mr. Marks turns with the dark, drab suit fabrics. He slowly rolls the lace, his disappointment palpable.)

Next time.

ESTHER: Mr. Marks?

MARKS: Yes?

(Esther wants to say something, but she can't quite find the words.)

Is there—?

ESTHER: No. No . . . I'm sorry . . . I can't do this. *(Distraught)* I thought I'd be able to, but I can't. I can't come here anymore. I—

MARKS: Why do you say this? Did I do something to offend, tell me, did I—

ESTHER: No.

MARKS: Then—

ESTHER: Please, I think you know why.

(A moment.)

MARKS: How many yards will you need for the gentleman's suit?

ESTHER: Four yards. The Scottish wool . . . and if you would, please wrap the Valenciennes lace.

(Lights crossfade to:)

SCENE 3

Rose Chemise

Light pours into Mrs. Van Buren's boudoir. Mrs. Van Buren sits on the bed cradling a snifter of brandy. She's upbeat, almost cheerful. Esther is distracted, however, consumed by her own thoughts.

MRS. VAN BUREN: He's gone to Europe.

ESTHER: I'm sorry to hear that.

MRS. VAN BUREN: You needn't be. It's a relief actually. Some business obligation. I don't expect to see him for months. He'll find ways of prolonging his stay, no doubt. Anyway, I'm considering a visit with friends in Lenox this summer. It'll be good to escape the city, don't you think? You could come, of course. I'll recommend your services to several women.

ESTHER: I thank you, but I can't. *(Drapes the Valenciennes lace over the bedpost)* Here. I found a strand of lace for your rose chemise. I know it ain't exactly what you wanted, but—

MRS. VAN BUREN: I had all but forgotten. I ordered it over four weeks
    ago. Four whole weeks. It's not like you to—
ESTHER: I been busy.
MRS. VAN BUREN: Oh? Indeed. How is our Mr. Armstrong?
ESTHER: Good. Well, he . . . good. Work scarce, and he so particular. He
    wanting, but his pride make him idle. And I try, I do, but he ain't
    really take to this city.
MRS. VAN BUREN: But he will. I am certain. Oh, Esther, it must be
    wonderful to be in love.
ESTHER: I suppose.

*(A moment. Mrs. Van Buren quickly examines the lace; indifferent, she
tosses it onto the bed. Esther bristles at her employer's lack of interest.)*

MRS. VAN BUREN: Is everything all right?
ESTHER: Yes.
MRS. VAN BUREN: Such a long face so early in the day. I won't allow it.

(Esther doesn't smile.)

Come.
ESTHER: I'd like to settle matters. Please. You ain't paid me in two
    months and I need the money.
MRS. VAN BUREN: Of course, I hadn't realized. *(Sits at her dressing table.
    Smiling to herself)* You know what? I miss writing our letters.
    I do! I've been absolutely without purpose for months.
ESTHER *(Snaps)*: Let's not talk about the letters!
MRS. VAN BUREN *(Surprised)*: Fine, we won't.
ESTHER: I'm sorry, Mrs. Van Buren.
MRS. VAN BUREN: Something is wrong.
ESTHER: No. Nothing.

*(Esther sits on the edge of Mrs. Van Buren's bed. She carefully refolds
the lace, attempting to hold back tears, but they come anyway.)*

MRS. VAN BUREN: Esther, what is it?

ESTHER: The other day George asked me to read a letter. I took it in my hand and I lied. I lie every day. And I'm a Christian woman.

(Mrs. Van Buren takes Esther's hand and sits down on the bed next to her.)

MRS. VAN BUREN: We do what we must, no? We are ridiculous creatures sometimes.

(A moment.)

ESTHER: Do you love Mr. Van Buren?

MRS. VAN BUREN: I am a married women, such a question is romantic.

ESTHER: But I fear my love belongs someplace else.

MRS. VAN BUREN: And why is that?

ESTHER: I shouldn't say. No, I can't. Perhaps I'm wrong.

MRS. VAN BUREN: Perhaps not.

(Mrs. Van Buren pulls Esther close and plants a kiss on Esther's lips. For a moment Esther gives in to the sensation of being touched, then abruptly pulls away, shocked.)

I'm sorry. I didn't mean to do that. I'm sorry. Please don't go. I just wanted to show you what it's like to be treated lovingly.

ESTHER: Don't say that. You don't love me.

MRS. VAN BUREN: How do you know? Please. We will forget this and continue to be friends.

ESTHER: Friends? How we friends? When I ain't never been through your front door. You love me? What of me do you love?

MRS. VAN BUREN: Esther, you are the only one who's been in my boudoir in all these months. And honestly, it's only in here with you that I feel . . . happy. Please, I want us to be friends.

ESTHER: I'm sorry. I can't.

MRS. VAN BUREN *(Screams)*: Coward!

(A moment.)

I'm sorry.

(Mrs. Van Buren digs into her dressing table drawer and produces a wad of money. She tosses the money on the bed.)

There.

ESTHER: I'm not the coward.

(Esther picks up the money.

Crossfade to Mayme's boudoir. Mayme plays a slow seductive rag. George enters. He watches Mayme gracefully regard the piano. He places money on top of the piano, then straddles the piano bench behind Mayme. He kisses her neck and cups her breasts in his hands.

Crossfade to Esther's bedroom. Esther sits alone, waiting.)

SCENE 4

Gentleman's Suit

Mayme's boudoir. Esther enters. Mayme is dressed in a red, flowing dressing gown. She bubbles over with excitement.

MAYME: I've saved up every penny I have. It's been two months and I want something new, Esther. Simple, this time, without all the pronouncement. Something a young gal might wear on her wedding night.

ESTHER: Wedding night? What ain't I heard? I don't believe those words got any place in your mouth.

MAYME: Seriously.

ESTHER: What's going on? C'mon, are you gonna tell me?

MAYME: It ain't nothing really. A fella, perhaps.

ESTHER: I thought you didn't feel nothing for these fools.

MAYME: Nothing ain't never felt so good.

ESTHER: Who is he?

MAYME: He ain't nobody really, but he real sweet. Like a schoolboy almost. We call him Songbird, 'cause he sing to speak. He come in like all them others. Hands crude and calloused, a week's wage in his pocket. But when we done, I didn't want him to leave, and I asked him to have a drink. Fool drunk up all my liquor, but it ain't bother me. In fact, I was fixin' to run out and git some more, but he placed his hands around my waist, real gentle and pulled me close. I actually wanted him to kiss me, I didn't even mind his sour tongue in my mouth, I wanted him there, inside me. He ain't like a lot of the colored men who pass through here with anger about their touch. He a gentleman. Comes three times a week on schedule, like the iceman. He was here last night until midnight, but he don't ever stay later. He just leaves his scent, which lingers until two A.M., or three, and I lie awake until it disappears.

ESTHER: He sounds wonderful.

MAYME *(Dubious)*: Yeah, I reckon.

ESTHER: What?

MAYME: Whatcha think—he got a wife. Yeah. A rich wife. But she troubles him, he say. Troubles him to no end. You should hear him go on about this poor gal. Made me feel bad for her.

ESTHER: She terrible, I'm sure. But just the same, you on uneasy ground.

MAYME: You find it shocking?

ESTHER: Yes, I find it shocking.

MAYME: Hush your mouth, you wouldn't understand. You want to see what my songbird give me?

(Mayme pulls George's Japanese smoking jacket from beneath her pillow. She displays it proudly.)

And you know me, I don't usually take gifts from men, but when he give me this, it took my breath away. It's so pretty. Look Esther. Feel it.

ESTHER *(Surprised)*: He give you this?

MAYME: Yup.

ESTHER: He must like you a bunch to give you something so fine.

MAYME: What can I tell you, the man got taste, honey.

ESTHER: I've only seen fabric like this just once before. It's Japanese silk.

MAYME: How'd you know?

ESTHER: It's expensive fabric. Very hard to find. You see the pictures were embroidered by an imperial artist, he signed it there. He give you this?

MAYME: He say I his gal. But this time a little part of me is hoping he telling the truth.

ESTHER: And what about his wife?

MAYME: What about her? I'm sure she just a sorry gal.

ESTHER: How you know she ain't a good person? And he just saying what you want to hear. That his words are a smooth tonic to make you give out what ain't free. How you know his wife ain't good?

MAYME: I don't know. But do it matter?

ESTHER: Yeah it do. You ever think about where they go after they leave here? Who washes their britches after they been soiled in your bed?

MAYME: No, I don't actually. Why would I?

ESTHER: 'Cause there's some poor woman out there waiting, getting up every five minutes, each time a carriage pass the window or a dog bark, who thinks a great deal of her husband, thinks so much of him that she don't bother to ask questions, she just know that there are places that he go that gentlewomen don't belong . . .

MAYME: I don't want to hear it!

ESTHER: She thinks he's playing cards or simply restless. But still, when the door opens and he lies down next to her, that poor stupid woman don't feel angry, because his body is warm and she ain't alone.

MAYME: What?! You troubled because he married? They all married. You ain't completely clean of this business. Truth. No, I don't care to think about those women. I don't care to think about the kind of lives that keep them sitting in their windows, worrying while their husbands—

ESTHER: I pity your heart. You are the worst sort of scavenger.

(Lights crossfade to George and Esther's bedroom. George stands in a new wool suit. Lights crossfade to Mayme's.)

MAYME: What's the matter with you?

ESTHER: I don't feel so good. That's all.

MAYME: I thought you'd be happy for me.

ESTHER: I think I'm gonna go home, if you don't mind.

(Lights crossfade to Esther and George's bedroom. George is in the new suit.)

GEORGE: Yuh t'ink I'd be taken for a Yankee gentleman? I do t'ink so, no? I'd like one them tall hats, whatcha call 'em? Like that fella across the way, yuh know, the one always be talkin' about 'e rich brother in Chicago. *(Affecting an American accent)* Yes, sir, my name George Armstrong and I from New York. Yes, sir, born here. *(Laughs)* It fit real nice. But, it seem to me that the fellas be wearin' shorter jackets with a touch of color.

(Esther pins George's pants.)

ESTHER: Sporting fellas, they ain't gentlemen. This Scottish wool. It white folk quality and it'll keep you warm through the winter. There is a lovely story—

GEORGE: Yeah? I'm sure it excitin'.

(Esther runs her hands down George's legs, then adjusts the hem. He does not respond to her touch.)

ESTHER: Be that way, I won't tell it then. There. You look good, George. Really. Now take off the pants so I can hem them proper.

GEORGE: Nah, don't bother. I need them for this evenin'.

ESTHER: This evening? Why? Don't go out. I bought fresh pork chops from Mrs. Franklin's son. I was gonna smother them in onions, the way you like. But it ain't worth the trouble if you ain't gonna eat. And . . . and I have something for you, I was going to save it for later . . . but . . . *(A moment)* Do you want to see?

GEORGE *(Excited)*: Sure.

ESTHER: Close your eyes. C'mon. And don't smile.

(George closes his eyes. Esther puts a rose in her hair and a touch of color on her lips. She nervously slips off her dress, revealing an elaborate corset similar to Mayme's.)

You can open your eyes.

(Esther awkwardly poses, awaiting George's reaction. His disappointment is palpable. He clearly was expecting something else. George chuckles to himself with a mixture of amusement and disgust.)

GEORGE: What yuh doing?
ESTHER: Don't you like it?
GEORGE: Come, put yuh clothin' on.
ESTHER: What's the matter? Ain't this to your liking? Ain't this what you want? *(Places George's hands around her waist)* Feel it. It satin. See?
GEORGE: No, don't do this, Esther. C'mon, this ain' yuh, 'ear.
ESTHER *(Timidly)*: If I ain't mistaken, a man has certain obligations. *(A moment)* Why won't you touch me?

(A moment.)

GEORGE: You want me to touch yuh?
ESTHER: Yes.

(George grabs Esther roughly around the waist. He plants a heavy, hard kiss on her mouth. She nevertheless succumbs to his touch.)

GEORGE: Like so? You want me to touch you. That all you want of George? You want me to bend and please, so you can feel mighty. No. *(George pushes Esther away)* 'Least in Panama a man know where 'e stand. 'E know 'e chattel. That as long as 'e have a goat 'e happy. 'E know when 'e drunk, 'e drunk, and there ain' no judgment if so. But then 'e drink in words of this woman. She tell 'e about the pretty avenues, she tell 'e plentiful. She fill up 'e head so it 'ave no taste for goat milk. She offer 'e the city stroke by stroke. She tantalize 'e with Yankee words. But 'e not find she. Only this woman 'ere, that say, "Touch me, George." And ask 'e to lie down on what she promise, lie down on 'e stable with a dozen strong horses for the work sites, ask 'e to lie down as they haul lumber and steel. Strong sturdy beasts. They are. 'E lie down, but what 'e get? No, he ain't gonna lie down no more.

ESTHER: Stop it. Why you talking this way?

GEORGE: I t'ink yuh know.

(A moment. George eyes the quilt.)

ESTHER: No. Please don't ask me again.

GEORGE: But it there dreamin' a fine fine house wit it own yard. It taunt 'e so, 'e can't even show what kind of man 'e be. What 'e hands can do.

ESTHER: No. That half my life. Thousands of tiny stitches and yards of fabric passed through that old machine.

GEORGE: And for what, huh? For it sit?

ESTHER: No.

GEORGE: Stop sayin' no! Ain't you see. If 'e own wife ain't willin' to believe in 'e, who will? 'E stand in work lines that wind around city blocks. But 'e don't have to no more, 'cause 'e know a fella got twelve draft horses and want to sell them quick quick. And 'e buy them, and in two years they'll have enough money for a beauty parlor even. They'll have the finest stable in New York City. People'll tip their hats and pay tribute. They'll call them Mr. and Mrs. Armstrong. The Armstrongs. Them church ladies will clear the front row just for them. And 'e will . . .

ESTHER *(Wants to believe him)*: He will what?

(George slowly moves toward Esther.)

GEORGE: 'E will sit with she and nod graciously to the ladies. 'E will come home for supper every evenin'. *(Seductively)* 'E will lie with she.

ESTHER: Only she?

(George strokes Esther's back tenderly; she savors his touch. He kisses her neck, her back, her shoulders, her breasts. He embraces her, almost too much. Esther nevertheless surrenders to the unexpected affection.)

Are you telling me the truth? Is this the truth?

GEORGE: Yes.

ESTHER: Please, you're not just saying that. You're not laughing at me
are you?

GEORGE: No, I ain' laughin'.

*(Finally, Esther breaks the embrace. She hesitates, then tears into the
quilt, wrenching it apart with her bare hands. She pulls the money out
and examines it, before placing it in George's outstretched hands.)*

ESTHER: There. There. There.

*(Esther's almost relieved to be shedding the money. Surprised, George
smiles and gathers the money into a pile.)*

GEORGE: So much 'ere. Sweet mercy, look at it all. Good lord, that
fella ain' gonna believe it. I gonna place the money square in 'e
hand, wipe that silly Yankee grin off 'e lips. I show 'e.

ESTHER: George, it's late, you ain't gotta do this now . . . put it back.
It'll still be there in the morning.

GEORGE: Woman, how yuh get so much?

ESTHER: Leave it. Come. George, I said put it back, it'll be there in the
morning! . . .

*(Esther beckons him to the bed. He looks at her pleading, outstretched
hand, but instead chooses to fetch a worn bag for the wrinkled money.
Esther, humiliated, studies her husband with growing horror. Aghast, she
slowly lowers her hand, and begins to put on her dress.)*

George?

(George continues to take unbridled delight in the money.)

George?

GEORGE *(Snaps)*: What?

ESTHER *(Whispered)*: Do you love me?

GEORGE: What the matter wit' you? You look as though you seen a
duppy.

ESTHER: Do I?

GEORGE: Why yuh look at me strange?

ESTHER: I asked you something.

GEORGE: Yuh my wife, ain't yuh?

ESTHER: Am I? *(Whispers)* I didn't write them letters.

GEORGE: I didn' hear what yuh said.

ESTHER *(Louder, almost too loud)*: I said I didn't write them letters.

(George studies Esther with disbelief.)

All this time I was afraid that you'd find me out. This good noble man from Panama. *(Retrieves a pile of letters tied with a satin ribbon)* I have all of your letters here. I look at them every day. I have one that looks as though it's weeping, because the words fade away into nothing, and another that looks as if it's been through a hard day, because there's a smudge of dirt at each corner, and it smells of kerosene and burnt sugar. But I can't tell you what it say, because I don't read. I can't tell whether there are any truths, but I keep them, 'cause George give me his heart, though it covered in mud and filthy, but he give it to me in one of these letters. And I believed him. I believed him! *(A moment)* But you ain't the man in these letters, because that gentleman would have thanked me. Who wrote them letters, George? Tell me!

(George considers.)

YOU TELL ME!

GEORGE: An old mulatto man. I paid him ten cents for each letter, ten cents extra for the fancy writing.

ESTHER: I ain't really Mrs. Armstrong, am I? I been holding on to that, and that woman ain't real. We more strangers now than on the eve of our wedding. At least I knew who I was back then. But I ain't gonna let you hurt that woman. No! She's a good decent woman and worthy. Worthy!

GEORGE: Esther!

(George reaches out to Esther.)

ESTHER: No, don't touch me! *(Backs away from George)*

GEORGE: Please. I ain' a thief. No. They warn't my words, but that don't mean I ain't feel them t'ings. I go now, and I gonna bring yuh back them horses.

ESTHER: I hope they real strong horses.

GEORGE: You'll see. And, we'll begin here.

(Lights crossfade to:)

SCENE 5

Smoking Jacket

Mayme's boudoir. Ragtime music plays, fast and furious. Mayme is lying on the bed wrapped in the Japanese smoking jacket. She sits up, pours herself a shot of moonshine and slams it back. A knock sounds on the door.

MAYME: Hold on, hold on.

(Mayme opens the door. Esther calmly enters. Mayme's unable to disguise her surprise.)

Esther! What . . . I got someone coming shortly. You can't stay.

(Mayme nervously wraps the smoking jacket around her body.)

I can't put him off. You understand. Come back later and we'll catch up.

(Esther grabs Mayme's arm.)

What's wrong?

(Esther gathers her strength.)

ESTHER: He gone.

MAYME: Who gone?

ESTHER: George.

MAYME: You ain't serious.

ESTHER: He has another woman.

MAYME: How do you know?

ESTHER: She told me so.

MAYME: She did? Well, she must be a cruel, heartless heifer.

ESTHER: You think so?

MAYME: Yes.

ESTHER: But, she ain't. When I left home this morning I intended to do harm to his whore. I was going to march into her room and scratch her face with my scissors. I was going to scar her. Make her ugly. Make her feel what I'm feeling. But she gonna know soon enough.

MAYME: You gotta go now.

ESTHER: No.

MAYME: Please, we'll talk about it later. I got someone coming.

ESTHER: Do you know what I done? I tore a hole in my quilt and give him my beauty parlor. Half my life bent at the machine, and I give it to him, just like that.

MAYME: Oh, Esther. Why?

ESTHER: I wanted to be held. *(Distracted)* I thought if . . . He ain't come home last night. I sat at the sewing machine all night, trying to make something. I just kept sewing together anything I could find until I had a strip a mile long, so long it fill up the apartment.

(A moment. Mayme runs her fingers along the fabric of the jacket.)

Do you know where he is, Mayme?

MAYME: Why would I know?

ESTHER: Because you're wearing the jacket I give him on our wedding night.

MAYME: How come you ain't say nothing before?!

(Horrified, Mayme rips off the jacket.)

ESTHER: What am I gonna say?

MAYME: Yeah, yeah. Last night Songbird come around the saloon in a new suit with bottomless pockets, throwing dice all night, and boasting of easy money. I ask him where he got the money, and he say his luck turn and he was gonna ride it out. If you can imagine that. He was gonna buy himself draft horses. The world changing and he wants big strong horses. He made me laugh. He promised to take me out someplace special, but I didn't have nothing nice to wear. And honestly it made me think about how long it been since I done something for myself. Gone someplace like you said, where a colored woman could go to put up her feet and get treated good for a change. And I see the dice rolling, and I think, Lord, God, wouldn't a place like that be wonderful? But every time the dice roll, that place is a little further away. Until it all gone.

And then I put my arms around this man, and I know who he is. He George. And maybe I known all along.

ESTHER: Why didn't you stop him?

MAYME: Because, he belong to me as well.

(Places the smoking jacket in Esther's hands) But this yours.

ESTHER: Foolish country gal.

MAYME: No, you are grand, Esther. And I ain't worthy of your forgiveness, nor will forget what you done for me. You ain't never treat me like a whore. Ever.

(George knocks on the door.)

ESTHER: Please don't answer that door.

(George knocks and rattles the door.)

Please don't, please don't answer.

MAYME: He's going to leave.

GEORGE *(Knocks and rattles the door more urgently; shouts)*: Mayme! *(Rattling the door)*

ESTHER: LET HIM GO!

(Mayme moves toward the door; Esther grabs her arm.)

Let him go. He ain't real, he a duppy, a spirit. We be chasing him forever.

(George knocks and rattles the door even more persistently. Eventually he stops. Silence. Mayme sits on her bed. Then Esther exits with the smoking jacket.
Lights crossfade to:)

SCENE 6

Japanese Silk

Mr. Marks's bedroom. Mr. Marks unfurls a roll of ocean blue fabric. As he turns, he finds himself facing Esther.

ESTHER: Hello, Mr. Marks.

MARKS *(Surprised)*: Miss Mills, I'm sorry, Mrs. Armstrong. How have you been?

ESTHER: I seen worse days. And you?

MARKS: I've seen better days. *(Laughs)*

ESTHER: I've been meaning to stop in. I walked past here a half dozen times trying to get up the courage to come in. You remember you sold me a rather special length of fabric some time ago.

MARKS: Please, remind me.

ESTHER: Japanese silk, with—

MARKS: Of course, I remember it.

ESTHER: Well, I made it into a man's smoking jacket, at your suggestion. *(Holds it up)*

MARKS: It is very nice, it will please your husband, I'm sure.

ESTHER: I want you to have it.

MARKS: Me? I can't—

ESTHER: Yes, you will.

(Mr. Marks accepts the jacket, genuinely touched by the gesture.)

MARKS: Thank you.
ESTHER: I can't stay. *(Begins to leave)*
MARKS: Wait, one moment.

(Mr. Marks removes his outer jacket, revealing the fringes of his tallit katan. He carefully puts on the silk jacket.)

What do you think?
ESTHER: It fits wonderfully.

(Esther takes a step toward Mr. Marks, hesitates, then takes another step forward. She raises her hands.)

May I?

(He nervously holds his breath, then nods yes. Esther reaches toward Mr. Marks, expecting him to move away. But he doesn't. She smoothes the shoulders of the garment, then expertly runs her hands down the jacket's lapels, straightening the wrinkled material. Mr. Marks does not move. Silence. Their eyes fix upon one another. Then Esther reluctantly walks away, exiting his bedroom without a word. Mr. Marks is left alone on stage. He contemplates the moment.

A gentle rag plays. Lights crossfade to Esther's bedroom at Mrs. Dickson's.)

SCENE 7

Patchwork Quilt

Mrs. Dickson's rooming house. Esther's old room. Mrs. Dickson folds laundry, humming a ragtime tune. Esther enters.

ESTHER: The girl downstairs told me I could find you up here.
MRS. DICKSON: My Lord, Mrs. Armstrong. I been telling everyone how you forgot us.

ESTHER: It ain't been that long.

MRS. DICKSON: Feel so.

(They hug.)

Look at you. I was about to take some tea. Come on into the kitchen, I'm glad for the company. These new girls are always out and about. They trouble me so these days, but whatcha gonna do? And I want to hear about everything.

ESTHER: Have you rented this room?

MRS. DICKSON: Why do you ask?

ESTHER: I don't much feel like saying why. If you please, just a yes or no would suit me fine.

MRS. DICKSON: No.

ESTHER: Well then, you won't mind another person at supper this evening. It's Friday, and you don't know how I been missing your carrot salad.

MRS. DICKSON: Of course. Esther—

ESTHER: I'm fine. *(Takes Mrs. Dickson's hand)* And I'd love that cup of tea.

MRS. DICKSON: Come on downstairs and we'll catch up. I'll tell you about Corinna Mae—girl's as big as a house, I swear to God.

(Esther, barely listening, takes in the room.)

She didn't waste any time getting pregnant and already talking nonsense about her man. When they first was married he was good enough for her, but to hear it now you'd think the man didn't have no kind of sense.

ESTHER: I don't care to hear about Corinna Mae.

MRS. DICKSON: Oh, I just thought—

ESTHER: I'd like to sit here for a moment.

MRS. DICKSON: Oh, yes. I gotta bring a few more things in off the line before the sunset. I'll see you downstairs shortly.

ESTHER: Of course. *(A moment)* Mrs. Dickson, thank you for not asking.

(Mrs. Dickson lovingly takes Esther's hand, giving it a supportive squeeze. She picks up the laundry basket and exits.

Esther lightly touches her belly. A moment. She walks over to the old sewing machine and begins to sew together pieces of fabric, the beginnings of a new quilt.

A slow, gentle rag plays in the distance. The lights shift, creating the quality of an old sepia-toned photograph. As the lights fade, a projected title card appears above Esther's head: "Unidentified Negro Seamstress, ca. 1905."

Blackout.)

END OF PLAY

FABULATION OR

The Re-Education of Undine

PRODUCTION HISTORY

Fabulation, or The Re-Education of Undine premiered at Playwrights
Horizons (Tim Sanford, Artistic Director; Leslie Marcus, Managing
Director; William Russo, General Manager) in New York City, on
June 13, 2004. It was directed by Kate Whoriskey; the set design was
by Walt Spangler, the costume design was by Kaye Voyce, the lighting
design was by David Weiner, the sound design was by Ken Travis and
the stage manager was Gillian Duncan. The cast was as follows:

UNDINE	Charlayne Woodard
STEPHIE/ENSEMBLE	Melle Powers
ACCOUNTANT RICHARD/ENSEMBLE	Stephen Kunken
HERVÉ/GUY/ENSEMBLE	Robert Montano
MOTHER/ENSEMBLE	Saidah Arrika Ekulona
FATHER/ENSEMBLE	Keith Randolph Smith
FLOW/ENSEMBLE	Daniel Breaker
GRANDMA/ENSEMBLE	Myra Lucretia Taylor

Characters

UNDINE

Ensemble

STEPHIE

ACCOUNTANT RICHARD

AGENT DUVA

HERVÉ

DR. KHDAIR

RAPPER

ALLISON

MOVERS

YORUBA PRIEST

MOTHER

FLOW

FATHER

GRANDMA

DRUG DEALER

OFFICER

INMATE #1 AND #2

GUARDS

JUDGE HENDERSON

ADDICTS

COUNSELOR

GUY

ROSA

DEVORA

GREGORY

CASEWORKER

SOCIAL SERVICES APPLICANTS

LANCE

YOUNG PREGNANT WOMAN

AN OBGYN DOCTOR

Time

The present.

Place

New York City.

Author's Note

The ensemble of four women and four men play multiple characters, with the exception of the actress playing Undine. The pace of the play should be rapid and fluid, allowing the scenes to blend seamlessly into each other without ever going to blackout until the end.

Ideally, the play should be presented without an intermission, but if necessary, one can be taken after Act 1, Scene 6.

Suggested doubling:

Guy/Hervé/Lance

Accountant Richard/Addict #1/Mover/Applicant/OBGYN doctor

Stephie/Counselor/Devora/Young pregnant woman/Applicant

Agent Duva/Flow/Rapper/Drug dealer/Mover/
  Addict ensemble/Applicant

Doctor Khdair/Grandma/Inmate #1/Caseworker

Allison/Mother/Rosa/Inmate #2/Addict ensemble/Applicant

Father/Gregory/Applicant/Officer/Yoruba Priest

Judge Henderson and the Guards can be played by any of the ensemble, male or female.

ACT ONE

SCENE I

Undine, a smartly dressed, thirty-seven-year-old African American woman, sits behind a large teak desk sporting a sleek telephone headset.

UNDINE: Can I be honest with you? I admire your expectations, but they're unrealistic, love. Yes, I can deliver something within your range. But your ambition outpaces your budget. But, but, listen to me, it's going to be a total waste of our energy. I've been doing this for a very long time. People give more when they get more, they want a seat next to a celebrity and a five-pound gift bag. It's the truth. Five years ago you could get away with half glasses of chardonnay and a musical theatre star, but not today. Generosity doesn't come cheaply. You're competing with heifers and amputees, rare palms and tuberculosis. What about the cause? Love, people don't want to think about a cause, that's why they give. Yes, I want to hear your thoughts, I am listening. *(She isn't)* Look, I'm at the outer limits of my time and so I'm going to ask you to speak more quickly. I will. Yes. We'll talk tomorrow about the new budget. Bye-bye.

(Undine hangs up and unfurls a self-satisfied smile. She buzzes her assistant.)

Stephie, if Altrice calls back, tell her I've left for the day. *(Excited)* Oh and did Hervé call? Buzz me when he does. *(Climbs onto the edge of her desk)* And sweet pea, where are we with tonight's event? Oh God, don't tell me that. You know the rule: if you can't get a celebrity, get me someone celebrity-like. Wait, wait I don't understand what you're saying. Stop, stop, stop. Get in here. *(To herself)* Okay, now how difficult is it to find me someone who can make an entrance?

(Stephie, a spacey twenty-something, enters in a very, very short light blue fur miniskirt.)

Jesus, how difficult is it? They can send probes to Mars, and I'm just asking for someone slightly fabulous.

STEPHIE: Like?

UNDINE: Like the fuck blond with the perky nipples. You know the one. She's what's-his-name's girlfriend. The comedian. You know. Her!

STEPHIE: She's an alcoholic, Undine.

UNDINE: So? The photographers adore her—

STEPHIE: She got sloppy drunk at the Wild Life benefit and puked on the buffet table.

UNDINE: I don't care if she's an alcoholic. As long as she can hold it together long enough for a photo-op. After that she can swim to Taiwan in booze for all I care.

STEPHIE: But—

UNDINE: Tell her it's an open bar, that way she'll get there on time.

STEPHIE: It . . . it doesn't feel right.

UNDINE: Oh it doesn't feel right? Visualize a job behind a counter, okay? How does that feel? Yeah, I thought so.

STEPHIE: Why are you being such a harpy this morning? You're acting like, I don't know a—

UNDINE *(Mimicking Stephie)*: An employer? Oh please, back to the list my little hater!

STEPHIE: I've been through the list like four times, I've called absolutely everyone.

UNDINE: What about the contingency list?

STEPHIE: Done.

UNDINE: What about—

STEPHIE: She's doing something with—

UNDINE: Fuck her, she hasn't had a movie in two years, two years and I'm offering her free publicity.

STEPHIE: Sorry, I spoke to her myself and she's like on some sort of spiritual—

UNDINE: Goddamn it, if I hear about one more celebrity on a spiritual journey I will, I will . . . It's okay, she's closed that door. Let her go. Let her go do her yoga thing, I don't care. So? How are we doing with our friends in the media?

STEPHIE: The perennial from WBAI and some intern from *Newsweek* confirmed, and everybody else is wait and see. Like, no one cares about fallopian blockage. It isn't exactly—

UNDINE: Hush! This is going to be fine. We're okay, we have plenty of time. Call George, tell him Undine is cashing in her favor. I need someone up-and-coming, young, hip. Hip-hop in fact. On the verge. Gangsterish enough to cause a stir, but not enough to cause a problem. And don't let him weasel out. I don't want *New York Times* hag-fest photos. Fun, fun, fun. *Vibe. Vanity Fair.* The V's. Let's mix and match a little bit, shake it up. Mix and match. Goddamn it, if we can't find a celebrity, we'll create a new one. This is going to be great. What are you wearing? *(Stephie starts to respond)* Good-bye!

STEPHIE: But—

UNDINE: Good-bye!

(Stephie moves to leave, then remembers something.)

STEPHIE: Oh I forgot, your accountant's waiting outside.

UNDINE: Oh God. What does he want? Give me a minute.

(Stephie leaves. Undine weeps uncontrollably. She stops abruptly, takes out a mirror, reapplies her lipstick, checks her teeth and wipes away the tears. Intercom:)

Send the little pussy in.

(The Accountant, Richard, an elegantly clad man in his mid-thirties, enters, shaking his head ever so slightly. All charm.)

Richard. Oh come on, it's little early in the day for a visit. Put away your business-school face. I'm not signing anything—
RICHARD: Why didn't you tell me you and Hervé split?
UNDINE: Why? Because I only just found out. Apparently I was the last to know.
RICHARD: Jesus, I'm sorry, Undine—
UNDINE: You? *(A moment)* How do you think I felt when I woke up this morning and his closet was bare?
RICHARD: Yikes, how'd he manage that?
UNDINE: I don't know, he took clothing to the dry cleaners every day. I didn't question it. I just thought he had a compulsion to be clean. Little ferret. How was I to know that he was slowly sneaking out of my life, piece by piece.
RICHARD: Do you know where he is?
UNDINE: Uh . . . No, and frankly I don't care.
RICHARD: Well, I wish you did.
UNDINE: We had dinner last night. I mean, we talked about redoing the living room in antique white. Stupid fucker. He was actually attentive and warm—
RICHARD *(Blurts out)*: And he was, well, he . . . Oooo . . . he was also slowly siphoning money out of your accounts.

(A moment.)

UNDINE *(Intercom)*: Stephie, would you come back in?
RICHARD: Undine, did you hear what I said?

(Stephie reenters.)

UNDINE: Sweet pea, will you have Jeremy run out and buy me some aspirin, a pregnancy-test kit. I also need a pair of panty hose, and tell that idiot that I don't wear flesh tone or natural. I'm suntan or bronzed or cocoa. Oh yes, and I desperately need a triple café latte, no milk.

STEPHIE: You mean a *(Italian accent)* triple espresso.

UNDINE: I'm so pleased you learned something during your year in Italia. How much did that word cost your parents, five hundred dollars? But what I'm asking for is a triple café latte with no milk. Is that clear?

STEPHIE *(Concerned)*: Are you all right? A little hateful today—

UNDINE: Embittered, sweet pea. It's the difference between cyanide and nicotine. I'm waiting for my coffee. Pronto. That's Italian for "do your job"!

STEPHIE: Is there anything else?

UNDINE: Stephie.

STEPHIE: Yes?

UNDINE: I love you. Good-bye!

(Stephie leaves.)

RICHARD: Undine, did you hear—

UNDINE: I don't believe it. He's a duplicitous conniving prick, but he's not a thief. Lighten up, he probably just took a cruise to Saint Martin's or moved the money into some mutual fund. He'll resurface when he gets bored.

(Richard laughs.)

RICHARD: Saint Martin's? I see. Shall I break it down for you? When you made your husband a cosignatory on all of your accounts, you essentially gave him the power to do whatever he wanted with your money. Which is exactly what has been done.

UNDINE: I'm sorry, my mind just went totally blank for a moment. Come again.

RICHARD: Undine, do you understand what I'm saying? He's absconded with all of your money.

UNDINE: Absconded? That's a very British word, Richard. You make it sound as if he's not coming back.

(Undine begins to laugh. Stephie reenters.)

RICHARD: I'm dead serious.

(Undine stops laughing.)

UNDINE *(To Stephie, curtly)*: What?
STEPHIE: I have the caterer on line one.
UNDINE: And?
STEPHIE: Your credit card, like, didn't go through. Sorry.
UNDINE *(Yelling)*: Sweet pea, I can't deal with this right now! Make it
   work.
STEPHIE: But—
UNDINE: Richard, how much are we talking about?
RICHARD: A lot.
UNDINE: How much?
RICHARD: A lot.
UNDINE: What's left?
RICHARD: Um . . . *(Shuffles some papers)* $47.51.
STEPHIE: Uh, the caterer's on the phone, um, like, she really needs to
   speak to you. What should I tell her?

(Richard lights a cigarette. Undine stands and paces.)

UNDINE *(To Richard)*: Goddamn it, why didn't you do something?
RICHARD: He's your husband. I did what you asked. I didn't want to
   step—
UNDINE: But you're my accountant. I mean, you've had dinner in my
   home. I bought a fucking five-thousand-dollar table at your
   wife's Blossom Buddy charity benefit. Good lord, I think we
   even got drunk once and made love in the men's room at
   Balthazar.

*(Stephie lets out a little gasp. Undine and Richard look away from each
other.)*

RICHARD: Um, I know the timing is awful but, Undine, we're going to
   have to consider bankruptcy. It's the only way to protect yourself. There isn't a stigma anymore.

UNDINE: What about that offer I had to sell to those bastards in Jersey?

RICHARD: I'm afraid that the bastards have rescinded their offer.

UNDINE: No. No. No. I don't want to talk about bankruptcy. I've spent fourteen years building this company. Bankruptcy—no. That implies that somehow I failed. Let me tell you something, Mr. Harvard M.B.A. My ancestors came shackled in wooden ships, crossed the Atlantic with nothing but memories! But I'll spare you my deprivation narrative. Let's just say their journey brought me here—their pain, their struggle, established me behind this fine expensive teak desk. It is teak, a strong and endangered wood. And now you want me to declare bankruptcy, because that Argentine prick has run off with my money.

RICHARD: Well, yes.

UNDINE: I will do what it takes. I will beg and borrow—but damn it, I'm not giving up my business. That's what I have, this is what I am. I will meet this month's bills, and take it from there—

RICHARD: It's not that simple.

UNDINE: All right, Richard, then make it simple.

RICHARD: You're broke, Undine, you're one month away from—

UNDINE: Goddamn it, don't say it.

(A man dressed in a plain blue suit enters.)

STEPHIE: Excuse me, but there's—

UNDINE: Why am I just finding this out now?

RICHARD *(Snaps)*: Because you don't bother to read your emails and you don't return phone calls. The truth is you haven't heard anything anyone has said in years!

STEPHIE: Uh—

UNDINE *(Annoyed beyond reason)*: What? What? What?

STEPHIE: There's a man who's been waiting—

RICHARD: Um, there is one other thing.

UNDINE: More?

RICHARD: Undine.

UNDINE *(To the man)*: Who the fuck are you?

RICHARD: This is—

AGENT DUVA: Agent Duva from the Federal Bureau of Investigation.

RICHARD: He'd like, um—

AGENT DUVA: To ask you a few questions.

RICHARD: I'm sorry, but this is about a little more than a spring shopping spree.

AGENT DUVA: Undine Barnes Call-es?

UNDINE *(Correcting)*: Calles. Yes.

AGENT DUVA *(Dramatically)*: FRAUD!

UNDINE: Excuse me?

AGENT DUVA: Perhaps you're familiar with the term "identity fraud"? You may not be aware, but we've been investigating your husband's activities for quite some time. I know this isn't easy for you—it never is. We will find him, I promise.

But beg my pardon for saying, there is one thing that troubles us about this . . . matter. Mrs. Calles, we've thoroughly searched our files, but our investigation can find no record of your existence prior to fourteen years ago. Undine Barnes Call-es, you seem to have materialized from the ether. We are not quite sure who you are.

UNDINE: Give me a moment. Please. That means step outside.

RICHARD, AGENT DUVA AND STEPHIE: Of course.

(Richard, Agent Duva and Stephie slip out. Undine lights a cigarette. Her right hand begins to shake slightly.)

UNDINE *(To audience)*: Actually, this is where the story will begin. It is mid-thought, I know, but it is the beginning. In the next twenty seconds I will experience a pain in my chest so severe, that I've given it a short, simple, ugly name—Edna. Forgive me, I *am* Undine Barnes Calles. Yes. I left home at thirteen. I was a bright child. I won a competitive scholarship through a "better chance" program to an elite boarding school in New England. I subsequently acquired a taste for things my provincial Brooklyn upbringing could no longer provide. I went to Dartmouth College, met and mingled with people in a constructive way, built a list of friends that would prove valuable years down the line. And my family . . . they tragically perished in a fire—at least that's what was reported in *Black Enterprise*. It was a misprint, but

I nevertheless embraced it as the truth. Fourteen years ago I opened my own very fierce boutique PR firm, catering to the vanity and confusion of the African American nouveau riche. And all seemed complete when I met my husband Hervé at a much too fabulous New Year's Eve party at a client's penthouse. Eleven months later we married.

(Hervé enters wearing a well-made suit and nursing a cocktail.)

Two years later he had a green card. Why? He permitted me to travel in circles I'd only read about in *Vanity Fair.*

HERVÉ *(Thick Argentinean accent):* Corfu, Milano, Barcelona, Rio.

UNDINE: He gave me flair and caché. What can I tell you? Hervé was dashing, lifted from some black-and-white film retrospective. He was a romantic. But before I introduce you to Hervé, I will now introduce you to Edna.

(Undine grabs her chest, gasping for air. Her face contorts with pain and she collapses against her desk.)

Stephie! Stephie.

(Lights come up on a doctor's office.)

SCENE 2

Dr. Khdair flicks on the examining room light. Undine sits on the examining table. Dr. Khdair carefully inspects the chart.

UNDINE: So. Am I dying?

DR. KHDAIR: No.

UNDINE *(Snaps):* What do you mean, "no"?

DR. KHDAIR: I thought you'd be relieved. I consider that good news.

UNDINE: Dr. Khdair, a heart attack at thirty-seven is never good news.

DR. KHDAIR: Well, you haven't had a heart attack.

UNDINE: Oh? *(Lighting a cigarette)* Then you won't mind if I have a little smoke.

DR. KHDAIR: Yes, actually I do. I wish you would stop.

UNDINE: Why? *(Dr. Khdair removes the cigarette from Undine's mouth)* So I can live to a ripe old age like some demure grandmother and face dementia, incontinence and a sagging ass? No thank you. I decided years ago never to view myself as a victim. Doctor, I'm thirty-seven in the age of terror, an early death seems merciful.

DR. KHDAIR: My God, that's tragic.

UNDINE: No, tragic is a crack-addicted woman breast-feeding her child. I'm far from tragic, thank you. Can I stand up?

DR. KHDAIR: No. Have you recently experienced any undue stress?

UNDINE: Like? Like if my husband left me suddenly, embezzling all of my money, leaving me on the brink of financial and social ruin?

(Dr. Khdair laughs thinking that Undine is kidding.)

DR. KHDAIR: You're very funny. Oh no, no, no. I'm talking about pressure at the job, an upcoming deadline, an important speech.

UNDINE: Work is work.

DR. KHDAIR: May I ask how much coffee you've had today?

UNDINE: Oh, I don't know three, maybe four, cups. I don't know. Is it important?

DR. KHDAIR: Well, yes. I believe you've suffered a severe anxiety attack. It's not uncommon.

UNDINE: Anxiety? Me? Oh no, I don't think so.

DR. KHDAIR: And why not?

UNDINE: Anxiety happens to weepy people on television newsmagazines.

DR. KHDAIR: Well, all of your tests came back normal. But there's one other thing Ms. Calles. I ran some routine tests and, congratulations, you're pregnant.

(A moment.)

UNDINE: Pregnant? *(To audience)* I met Hervé at a dinner party three years ago. He was standing by the crudités, dipping broccoli spears into the dip.

(Hervé enters. He wears his well-made suit. He moves with the grace of a flamenco dancer. He holds a broccoli spear between his fingers.)

He did it with such flair that I found myself hovering around the hors d'oeuvres table for most of the evening. I watched, dazzled, as he sucked the dill dip off the vegetable with his full lips.

(He pops the broccoli spear into his mouth and wipes his lips with a napkin.)

Up until then I'd been dating a rapper at the twilight of his career.

(Rapper boyfriend enters.)

He'd become addicted to painkillers and his paranoia was making the relationship tiresome. He'd drive around Bushwick, Brooklyn, in his SUV, tunes pumping, yearning for ghetto authenticity. His six-figure income had isolated him from the folks. But nevertheless, he was becoming more ghetto by the moment. Too ghetto for the ghetto.

(Hervé gazes at Undine; their eyes lock.)

Hervé looked over at me—I was five, I was twelve, I was seventeen, I was twenty-eight. I explored the full range of my sexual awakening in that moment. As he approached, I could not move my feet, and actually felt something I read a million times in romance novels: a tingle in my loins.

HERVÉ *(With his thick Argentinean accent)*: Hello.

UNDINE: Hello. Did you enjoy the dip? *(To audience)* I could think of nothing cleverer to say and averted my gaze. Then I glanced at my boyfriend with the hostess and a Philly Blunt between his fingers. And I channeled all the charm in the universe.

(Rapper boyfriend retreats into darkness.)

(To Hervé) It is almost midnight and I see that you're alone.

HERVÉ: Yes, it appears so.

(A slow tango begins to play.)

UNDINE: Have you seen the view from the balcony? It is spectacular.

HERVÉ: Yes . . . I have . . . seen . . . the view, and it is spectacular. Could I interest you in a dance? *(Extends his hand; he pulls Undine in close)*

UNDINE *(Breathless)*: What is this music?

HERVÉ: You have never heard of Andrés Segovia?

UNDINE: No.

(They begin to tango.)

HERVÉ: *Por qué?* He is a master of classical guitar from *España.* The best, of course. He found a way to isolate emotion with his fingers. *(Leads Undine through a series of elaborate dance steps)* What he can do with a series of chords . . . is remarkable. I fell in love with his music in Madrid. I was curating an exhibition of important artists in *España.* I had the good fortune of dining in a café with the brilliant artist Ernesto Pérez. The music began. The guitar. A recording of Segovia's music. The place fell silent. We listened, intensely, for with a mere guitar he created an orchestra, indeed from those most basic chords he wove something so marvelously complicated that it made us ashamed of our own limitations. In that small café Segovia opened up possibility. *Querida,* I can't believe you don't know his music.

(The music ends. Hervé kisses Undine's hand.)

UNDINE *(To audience)*: And with a handful of words, I had fallen in love.

(Hervé exits.
   Lights bring us back to Undine's office.)

Scene 3

Allison, a well-turned-out African American woman, enters Undine's office with two glasses and a bottle of wine. She speaks with an affected continental accent and carries herself with great poise and self-importance. Actually, she struts.

ALLISON: Did you tell him? Does he know?
UNDINE: No.

(Allison sits on Undine's teak desk.)

ALLISON: What are you going to do?
UNDINE: Exercise my constitutional right.
ALLISON: He doesn't deserve to be a father—
UNDINE: Or a husband—
ALLISON: Bastard—
UNDINE: Oh God, why did I have to get pregnant?
ALLISON: Don't speak to me about fertility. Look at me—I'm on hormone cocktails, and it is hideous.
UNDINE: But you don't want a child, Allison.
ALLISON: Of course I don't. But everyone else is doing it, and you know Daryl, he won't be left behind.

(Allison unfolds the Daily News *and holds it out to Undine.)*

Here. I brought you the *Daily News.* Page four. I thought you might—
UNDINE: I have it—
ALLISON: Did you see the photo that they used?
UNDINE: No kidding.
ALLISON: Terrible. You're not that heavy, darling.
UNDINE: Fraud! Can you believe that Argentine testicle was breaking the law on my nickel?
ALLISON: Don't talk to me about it. I've been there with Daryl and the whole brokerage house scandal. Page two, three days running. I don't want to relive those years. I had to scratch and claw

my way back onto party lists and even now around Christmas the mailbox isn't nearly as full. There is nothing less forgiving than bourgie Negroes.

UNDINE: Who are you telling? My phone has stopped ringing— I even called the phone company to see whether it had been disconnected, that's how silent it's been. I've become some sort of social pariah—people act as if the mere presence of my voice on an answering service is enough to sully their reputation. I've called everyone: Diane Madison, Ken Brooks, Sylvia Foster-McKay.

ALLISON: Sylvia?

(Movers enter. Throughout the rest of the scene they slowly disassemble Undine's office.)

UNDINE: Yes. Most people never got back to me, and those that did seemed frightened by my predicament. Jesus Christ, you're the only friend who's bothered to stop by.

ALLISON *(Surprised)*: Is that so?

UNDINE: No one seems troubled by the actual charges against me. No, the crime isn't being a criminal, it's being broke. It's apparently against the law to be a poor black woman in New York City.

ALLISON *(Shocked)*: You're broke, darling? You didn't tell me that. *(Truly disturbed by this revelation)*

UNDINE: Yes. *(Whispers)* They auctioned off my furniture; it was like a feeding frenzy, people I knew bidding on my possessions, waving little flags and purchasing bits and pieces of my life for a bargain.

ALLISON: Vultures.

UNDINE: At some point I thought they were actually going to put *me* up on the block and sell me to the highest bidder. And in a flash I thought, Thank God I got my teeth done last year. "Look at them teeth, she got a fine set of teeth, y'all." How naïve, foolish of me, to assume that I was worthy of some comfort and good fortune, a better chance. They give you a taste, "How ya like it?" then promptly take it away. "Oh, I'm sorry, we've reached our quota of Negroes in the privileged class, unfortunately we're bumping you down to working class." Working. I'm not even working. I think I'm officially part of the underclass. Penniless. I've returned to my original Negro state.

ALLISON: Enough! This talk is unsettling me. I need a glass of wine.
(Pours them each a glass of wine)

UNDINE: I'm sorry, Allison. I didn't mean to burden you with all of this. I'm really glad you came. *(Taking in her empty office)* Look at this, a lifetime of hard work, and here I am on the verge of becoming a statistic. And damn it, I don't want a child. Not like this. Fuck him! I took vows. Two years, ten months and twelve days.

ALLISON: You could always marry that client of yours, the rapper, what's his name? Mo' Dough.

UNDINE: Yeah, and be a gangster bitch, a chicken head, no thank you. The money wouldn't last, and really is there anything more pathetic than an aging broke b-boy who ain't got no rap left.

ALLISON: Then what you are you going to do?

UNDINE: I don't know! Don't ask me. Maybe I'll go to church or give alms. I'll climb a mountain or tend to some limbless African children in the middle of a malaria zone.

(They share a laugh at the notion.)

And by the way, when did you acquire that fabulous accent?

ALLISON: Do you like it?

UNDINE: Yes. I love it.

ALLISON: Good. I've been trying it out. I'm in my Eartha Kitt phase, I'm making bold social choices. You don't think it's too much?

UNDINE: Of course it is. But you do your thing, girl. *(To audience)* Allison, known in Harlem as Tameka Jo Greene, aspired to the black bourgeoisie after a family trip to New Rochelle. She managed to transcend her modest childhood in the Langston Hughes public houses. Yes, a member of a Hundred Black Women, owns a house on Martha's Vineyard and an apartment on the Upper East Side (the low seventies). Then her husband appeared naked in a gay porn magazine, and the youthful indiscretion stripped her of her social status. But I admire her tenacity. It is an unrelenting struggle to regain social favor. And God bless her, she's on hormones and on the verge of a reemergence.

ALLISON: I'm your best friend. Whatever you need, I'm here.

UNDINE: I have to move out of my apartment. May I stay with—

ALLISON *(Dropping all affect)*: Oh no girl, we'd love to have you, but you know, we're in the process of renovating. *(Restoring the affect)* It's absolutely crazy. Listen, when we finish the new place on the Vineyard. You're welcome.

UNDINE: Thank you, but I've been told I can't leave New York, at least not until the investigation is complete. And Allison, I'm clinging to my last few dollars—

ALLISON: My goodness, look at the time.

UNDINE: You have to leave so soon?

ALLISON: I'm having lunch with . . . Sylvia.

UNDINE: Sylvia?

ALLISON: Yes, but we'll have dinner soon.

UNDINE: Soon.

ALLISON: Promise.

UNDINE: Promise.

(Allison heads for the door; she stops herself.)

ALLISON *(Dropping the affect)*: Undine, you understand.

(Allison exits. A Yoruba Priest, dressed in white, enters carrying a candle and a Nigerian divination board. He speaks with a rich Nigerian accent.)

YORUBA PRIEST: The spirits are speaking. The door to all roads is open.

UNDINE *(To audience)*: Richard, my accountant, recommended I see a Yoruba priest. It was his parting advice on coping with my predicament. They were roommates at Harvard Business School. So I thought, Why not?

(The Yoruba Priest does a short chant and throws out a handful of cowrie shells on a divination board.)

YORUBA PRIEST: It seems you've angered Elegba, the keeper of the gate. He opens the doors to the spiritual world. He's one of the trickiest and most cunning *orishas*.

UNDINE: Okay, so what does that mean?

YORUBA PRIEST: He's quite furious from what I see here.

UNDINE: Why on earth is Elegba angry at me? What have I ever done to the African spirits?

(The Yoruba Priest throws out another handful of cowrie shells on the divination board.)

YORUBA PRIEST *(Surprised and concerned)*: Oh?

UNDINE: What? What do you see?

YORUBA PRIEST: It's what I thought. You have a bit of work to do in order to placate Elegba.

UNDINE: Work? Like what?

YORUBA PRIEST: He says it's been a long time since you've been home. And as such you must give him a thousand dollars and a bottle of Mount Gay premium rum.

UNDINE: What? You gotta be kidding. That's— *(Examines the cowries)*

YORUBA PRIEST: Oh no. He's one of the most unpredictable and demanding orishas. It's a symbolic offering, an appeasement. But—

UNDINE: Will he accept a heartfelt apology? I mean, really, what is Elegba going to do with a thousand dollars?

YORUBA PRIEST: I don't ask, I interpret. But I've experienced his wrath and believe me, if I were you, I'd pay the spirit.

UNDINE: Will he take a check?

(The Yoruba Priest throws out the cowrie shells, reads the configuration.)

YORUBA PRIEST: No. Cash only. Kneel and repeat after me. Elegba, open this door—

(Undine kneels next to the Yoruba Priest. He passes Undine a cigar.)

UNDINE *(To audience)*: I am taking no chances. *Ashé.* I lay my last thousand dollars at the altar of an angry African spirit, light a candle, smoke a Macanudo, and on the advice of a spirit, I reluctantly return to my last known address in Brooklyn.

(Lights crossfade to a dining room.)

SCENE 4

The Walt Whitman projects. Undine's family. Mother, Father and Grandma are straightforward no-nonsense people. Her brother, Flow, is a hipster with a tatty Afro and goatee. He has the habit of speaking a bit too loudly. They all wear security guard uniforms, except Grandma, who wears a brightly colored Conway housecoat. Grandma, regrettably, is confined to a wheelchair. The family sits around the kitchen table without speaking. Father places the Daily News *on the table and takes a long swig from a large can of malt liquor.*

UNDINE: So, can I stay here until I get back on my feet?
MOTHER: Let me get this straight—you want to stay here? Here?
UNDINE: Um, yes.

> *(Mother looks to the others; they all look back at Undine.)*

MOTHER: But I thought you didn't do public housing.
UNDINE: Did I say that? I don't recall.
MOTHER: Well, the elevator don't work, there ain't been hot water since May and some fool's been flashing his ass at the ladies in the stairwell, but I suppose we got the room.
UNDINE *(Forced)*: Wonderful.

> *(Uncomfortable silence.)*

It's all right for us to speak.

> *(A moment. Silence.)*

FLOW: So.
UNDINE: Yes?
FLOW: You bugged out.
MOTHER: Shhh. Your sister's come home for a little rest and relaxation.
FLOW: What the fuck? Club Med was overbooked?
MOTHER: Shhh. Shhh.
FLOW: You ain't been here for years, and you just decided to stop in for a little R and R—forgive my skepticism and tone of disbe-

lief. I'm going to laugh real hard and long for moment. *(Bursts into laughter)*

UNDINE: At least I left, Flow. Are you still working on the epic poem about Brer Rabbit?

FLOW *(Suddenly serious, without a breath)*: It is the exploration of the African American's journey. I'm exploring the role of the trickster in American mythology. I am using Brer Rabbit, classic trickster, as means to express the dilemma faced by cultural stereotyping and the role it plays in the oppression on one hand and the liberation of the neo-Afric (to coin a phrase) individual, on the other. We at once reject and embrace—

UNDINE *(To audience)*: Flow was never the same after his tour of Desert Storm. I know it's a cliché, but something did happen to him in the desert. Military school, a year at West Point, the Green Berets and finally a security guard at Walgreen's. He couldn't ever reconcile his love of the uniform with his quest for personal freedom. Hence the poem.

FLOW: It is this very conundrum that intrigues and confounds. We love, but we despise him. We admire, yet rebuke. We embrace, yet we push away. This glorious duality enlivens and imprisons him. Because ain't he only hunting for "a way out of no way," as it's been said. And so you know, the poem is not about Brer Rabbit, he is merely a means to convey a truth—

FATHER *(Urging Flow on)*: Speak!

(Grandma nods off at the dinner table. Mother loses herself in a book of word search puzzles.)

FLOW: It is open-ended. A work in progress. A continuous journey. Oh shit, what time is it? They just got in the new Epilady and all the little motherfucking thieves'll be in tonight. I gotta roll in ten. *(Puts on his security utility belt)*

MOTHER: So, how long are you going to be with us? *(Looks up from her word search)*

UNDINE: Not long.

MOTHER: Well, I hope you don't mind sharing the bed with Grandma. I'll turn the mattress before you go to sleep.

UNDINE: That's okay, I'll manage.

FATHER: Shiiiiit.

UNDINE: Excuse me?

FATHER: You know Velvet Whitehead dead.

MOTHER: What?

UNDINE: Who's Velvet Whitehead?

FATHER: Snookie's cousin's brother's father. You know Velvet solved that mathematical problem yesterday. That equation they be talking about in the big paper. That problem all them scientists—

UNDINE: Mathematicians—

FATHER: —been 'rassling with.

UNDINE: Yeah, right.

FATHER: Fifty-thousand-dollar award for solving it.

FLOW: What?

MOTHER: Velvet Whitehead?

FATHER: Yesterday. We was sitting up in Cellars restaurant and he said, "Let me see that shit." Yes, he did. It took the brother all of ten minutes; he wrote the solution out on a napkin.

FLOW: Smart brother. Did two years at Stony Brook.

FATHER: Read the *New York Times* every mutherfucking day, subscribed to the *Economist*. The *Economist*—that's a magazine from England.

UNDINE: Yes, I'm familiar with England, I've actually *(Affecting a British accent)* been.

FATHER: You been to England?

FLOW: But you ain't *(Affecting a British accent)* been home.

FATHER: But our Velvet was an around-the-way brother. Real. You know, could talk some talk like he was theoretician, and a minute later be bullshitting with some crazy-ass fool on the corner.

MOTHER: I bet Gloria is all torn up.

FATHER: Velvet saw the equation on the page, little printed X's and numbers—and bam—the solution revealed itself. It was a wonder to watch the brother work. His brain was like Coltrane on the sax, you know. *(Scats)* 1, 2, 3, 7, 9, 6, 13. *(Scats like numbers are tumbling out of his mouth)* He kept decades' worth of shit in his head—spreadsheets, numbers, birthdays, deaths—a statistical oasis. Yeah. He wrote out the solution like it was a phone number, drank down his beer, sucked the last bit of meat off his spare ribs, and talked about he was going to step outside for a smoke. I picked up the napkin, and I saw it, jack. Little numbers and letters, written in perfect Catholic-school hand. We was laughing, 'cause we had already spent his fifty thousand dollars, when we heard the gunshot. BAM! By the time we ran outside Velvet was dead. A bullet to the right side of his head. Yeah, baby, they knocked his cerebellum clear out his skull, splattered onto the parking meter with ten minutes left. And I went back inside to call the ambulance and the waitress was wiping up the table with Velvet's solution. Easy come, easy go, baby.

UNDINE: I don't want to rain on your parade, but how do you know he really solved the problem?

FATHER: 'Cause he did. *(With intensity)* He looked at it, jack . . . And I saw it in his gaze, it was there for him. Absolute clarity. He talked about how white folks overcomplicate things by not seeing the basic formula and rhythm of life. I tell you, the solution was there as plain as the truth. It was the truth. And I believed him. They'll have us believe that the problem can't be solved, that it ain't even within our grasp. So a nigger don't even bother to reach. But there are brothers like Velvet all over this city.

FLOW: That's right!

FATHER: I met brothers in 'Nam that should have been generals, but left with an enlisted man's pension. That's what I'm talking about. Velvet solved that problem, baby.

UNDINE: You're a trusting friend. A folded *New York Times* and some scribbles on a napkin—with such faith you'd think there'd be no more problems in the world.

FLOW: What do you know with your bootleg ideas?

UNDINE: I know a fifty-thousand-dollar problem isn't solved on a napkin. I know something isn't so because you want it to be so. I mean, I'm sorry to hear about Velvet, I am. But I didn't come all the way home to talk about him. *(A moment)* How are *you*, Daddy?

FATHER: I is and sometimes I ain't. *(Shrugs his shoulders)*

UNDINE *(To audience)*: My family. The fire victims. Mother and Father good hardworking people. They took the police exam six times back in the seventies, before they realized the city wasn't going to let them pass. They settled into a life as security guards at Long Island University, hence the uniforms. It is a safe home.

MOTHER (*Circling a word in her word search*): "Relief." Look at that.

UNDINE: What are you working on, Mom?

MOTHER: Word search. Just finished my third book this week.

FLOW: So where's the baby daddy? What he gots to say about all this?

UNDINE: Isn't it time for your jackass pill?

MOTHER: Will you two please? Stop it! We're happy to have you home, Sharona. You stay as long as you want. There's plenty of room.

UNDINE: Mom, it's Undine.

MOTHER: I forgot, Undine, you gonna have to be patient.

FLOW: Well, I ain' calling her Undine. If it was Akua or Nzingha, a proud African queen, I'd be down with it. But you are the only sister I know that gots to change her beautiful African name to a European brand.

UNDINE: Correct me if I'm wrong, but you weren't exactly born with the name Flow. So shut up. (*Grandma audibly exhales, and nods out*) What's wrong with Grandma?

MOTHER: She's just a little tired. Sometimes she nods off, the diabetes is taking its toll.

UNDINE (*Loudly*): Are you all right, Grandma?

MOTHER: She's fine, just let her be.

(*A moment. Undine's breathing becomes labored. Anxiety.*)

UNDINE (*To family*): Excuse me. I'm feeling a little nauseous.

MOTHER: If you're going to the bathroom, take Grandma with you.

(*The lights crossfade; we're now in Grandma's bedroom.*)

SCENE 5

Grandma, all warmth and care, sits in her wheelchair crocheting a doily or something like that. Undine rests on the arm of the chair.

GRANDMA: You look good, Sharona.

UNDINE: I don't feel so.

GRANDMA *(Taking Undine's arm)*: You got that glow. A woman with child, ain't nothing more beautiful.

(Undine recoils.)

Sweet pea, I been hoping you'd come home. I think about you a lot.

UNDINE: Nobody else seems particularly happy to have me back.

GRANDMA: Don't let them fool you, you they prize heifer. And sweet pea, you don't know how these folks brag on you.

UNDINE: I hope you don't mind that I'm sharing your room.

GRANDMA: Bet it ain't as beautiful as your apartment, but it got a lovely view of the next building. I've counted the number of bricks, sixty-three thousand and ten . . . What happened, Sharona?

UNDINE: It went away.

GRANDMA: Things don't just go away. They get taken away, they get driven away, they get thrown away.

UNDINE: All of the above.

GRANDMA: June seventeenth. It was an unseasonably cold day. You walked out that door in a dark green linen suit, orange silk shirt, and never walked back through, until now.

UNDINE: I had to. And c'mon, you didn't expect me to come back?

GRANDMA: A visit, yes.

UNDINE: You have been getting my Christmas cards?

GRANDMA: Your Christmas cards are always lovely. If they didn't come every year I'd think you fell off the earth.

UNDINE: I've been very busy. If you knew—

GRANDMA: A year I can forgive, but it has been nearly fourteen.

UNDINE: Fourteen? My God. Fourteen years. I really wasn't aware that that much time had passed. Honestly. Time just passed. It did.

GRANDMA: Are you ashamed of us?

UNDINE: No.

GRANDMA: But, you ain't telling the truth. Sweet pea, why'd you come home?

UNDINE: I don't know what to say other than a month ago I sat in my doctor's office and she told me I wasn't dying and I was actually disappointed. Grandma, I wanted to—

(Grandma tenderly grasps Undine, but her hands begin to shake ever so lightly.)

What's wrong?

GRANDMA: Bad habits.

UNDINE: Are you all right, Grandma?

GRANDMA: Yes. No. Would you hand me that bag? I need my medicine.

(Undine lifts up a paper bag. The contents tumble out into Grandma's lap: a baggie of white powder, a box of matches, a hypodermic needle, a spoon and a tourniquet.)

UNDINE: What is this?

GRANDMA: What it look like?

UNDINE: Is this stuff Flow's? Oh no, don't tell me he's using heroin.

GRANDMA: Why would you think that? Flow is trouble, but he is a good man.

UNDINE: This belongs to somebody.

GRANDMA: I be that somebody.

UNDINE: You?

(Grandma's hand shakes as she rolls up her sleeve. Bruises line her arm.)

(Horrified) Grandma, how long have you been shooting heroin?

GRANDMA: Since your grandfather died, baby girl.

UNDINE: Does Mommy know?

GRANDMA: If she do, she ain't said nothing.

(A hypodermic needle tumbles to the ground.)

UNDINE: I don't believe it.

GRANDMA: Pass me my works.

UNDINE *(Undine picks up the needle and Grandma snatches it from her hand)*: This is crazy.

GRANDMA: Change be what it will. I'd say it were crazy if it wasn't so necessary.

(She goes through the process of preparing heroin.)

UNDINE: You nearly beat me down when you caught me smoking herb with Omar Padillo.

GRANDMA: Well, some things have happened since then. I got good and old for one. They think I'm diabetic. Your idiot brother even gives me the injections, my hands shake so bad these days.

UNDINE: I'm not going to watch you do this.

GRANDMA: I wish you wouldn't. *(Tightens the tourniquet)* Sweet pea, I thought that I'd get to this point and be filled with so much wisdom that I'd know just how to control the pain that's trailed me through life. The truth would be revealed, and some great doorway would open and God's light would encircle and lift me out of the ordinariness of my life. One would think you'd be closer to God at my age, but I find myself curiously further away.

UNDINE: How can you say that?

GRANDMA *(Emphatic)*: I'm old. I can't do it, Sharona. I ain't happy. What do I get to look forward to each morning? The view that brick building across the way and perpetually gray life. For a few dollars I get to leave this drab apartment. Who is hurt? At your age I already had five children. I did for others so long—well, now it's time to do for myself.

(Grandma turns away from Undine and injects herself with heroin. She slips into a heroin-induced languor, a junkie nod. She appears to be defying gravity as she leans forward in her chair. Just as she seems on the verge of falling out of the chair, she miraculously recovers. Undine watches, horrified, as her mother enters carrying a cup of hot chocolate.)

MOTHER: I thought you might want some hot chocolate.

UNDINE: Do you know that Grandma is shooting heroin?

MOTHER: You always had an active imagination. *(Props Grandma up in the chair)*

UNDINE *(To audience)*: And this concludes the section entitled "Denial and Other Opiates."

MOTHER: She'll be all right, it's the sugar. *(Gives Grandma a kiss and exits)*

UNDINE: Grandma, Grandma.

GRANDMA: Yes, baby. Will you do me a favor?

UNDINE: Yes, of course.

GRANDMA: I need you to go out and get me some white lace.

UNDINE: What?

GRANDMA: My legs all swollen up, barely walk. But I'm gonna need another fix soon enough.

UNDINE: No, I'm not going to do it. I'm not. I refuse. No.

GRANDMA: You want me to die? That what you want? *(Shouts)* I don't need no moralizing, I need smack and I need it now.

UNDINE: I don't even know where to get it.

GRANDMA: On the corner of—

UNDINE *(To audience)*: One A.M., Saturday night. My entire life has been engineered to avoid this very moment.

(Undine sheepishly approaches a Drug Dealer lingering on the corner. She looks from side to side for some invisible jury.)

Excuse me.

DEALER: What?

UNDINE: I'd like one hundred dollars of *(Whispers)* white trace, please.

DEALER: What?

UNDINE: White taste. White lace. Fuck. Heroin!

DEALER: Do I know you?

UNDINE: No, and that's how I'd like to keep it.

DEALER: Are you a cop?

UNDINE: No. Are you a dealer?

DEALER: You sure you ain't a cop?

UNDINE: Would you like me to fill out a questionnaire? Let's cut the bullshit—I'm not buying a condo. Just give me the goddamn drugs— *(Thrusts money in his direction)*

DEALER: Bitch, put the money down, this ain't a fucking supermarket.

UNDINE: Listen, friend, this is humiliating enough without the insults. Can I give you a little business tip? If you treat your customers with respect, they'll give you a little respect in return.

DEALER: My customers are junkies, I ain't need they respect.

UNDINE: For the record, I'm not a junkie.

DEALER: Oh you ain't a junkie, you just copping dope for a friend.

UNDINE: Yes, as a matter of fact.

DEALER: Bitch, give me the money. And get your tired junkie ass out my face.

UNDINE: You call me bitch one more time and I just might take my business elsewhere.

DEALER: Take it elsewhere. Bitch!

UNDINE: My man, there is no need to resort to some ghetto drug dealer cliché. It's late, I'm not going to wander through this neighborhood looking for drugs, that's not my ideal Saturday evening out. So let's just wrap up this little interaction.

DEALER: Show me the dollars, and get the fuck out of here!

(Undine slips the Dealer the money; he gives her the drugs.)

Ho! 5-0!

(Police sirens blare; the Dealer tosses the heroin at Undine and runs. A flashlight hits Undine, who freezes like a deer caught in headlights. The Dealer has disappeared.)

UNDINE *(To audience)*: When you read the newspaper tomorrow and wonder, "How does it happen?" Now you know. One evening you're at a gala celebrating the opening of an expensive new museum wing, and the next you're standing on a street corner with a hundred dollars worth of heroin and a flashlight shining in your face.

OFFICER: Arms where I can see them.

UNDINE: Officer, I know this may sound ridiculous, but this is not my heroin. *(Drops the bag of heroin)* I bought it for my grandmother.

OFFICER: State your name.

UNDINE: Undine Barnes Calles.

OFFICER: Do you have anything that's gonna stick me?

UNDINE: No.

OFFICER: Miss Calles, you have the right to remain silent. Anything—

(A photo is snapped. Camera flashes. Undine turns to the side. Camera flashes again. Undine is forcefully led to a prison cell occupied by two other women.)

SCENE 6

Undine stands apart from the other women in the prison cell. She steals a glance at Inmate #1, a hardened, butch woman who speaks in a harsh, biting tone.

INMATE #1: Find what you looking for?

(*Undine self-consciously averts her gaze, and does not respond.*)

You ain't hear me? Yeah, you.

UNDINE: Excuse me, are you talking to me?

INMATE #1: Who else I be talking to?

UNDINE (*Under her breath*): I don't know, someone else, hopefully.

INMATE #1: What did you say?

UNDINE: Nothing.

INMATE #1: Don't make me have to come over there and teach you how to crawl. What, you think you special? There ain't no real Gucci here. This the markdown rack, bitch.

(*Undine digs in her bag, puts on a pair of dark Gucci sunglasses and turns away.*)

Don't turn your head like I owe you money. Shit, you don't know me. (*Laughs with bravado*)

UNDINE: No.

INMATE #1: No, what?

UNDINE: No. I don't know you. And if I was looking at you, I wasn't aware of it. I'm sorry.

INMATE #1: Oh, you sorry?

UNDINE: Yes, I'm sorry.

INMATE #1: That's right, you sorry.

(*Inmate #1 gets in Undine's face.*)

UNDINE: Yes, I'm sorry. I'm sorry that I looked at you. Okay? I'm sorry that you're so angry, I'm sorry that we're stuck here in the middle of the fucking night. I'm sorry for a whole series of things that are far too complicated to explain right now, and I'M SORRY, THAT I'M SORRY. *(Unhinged)* So if you don't mind, I'm going to move to the other side of this . . . cell and sit quietly until they call my name. If you want to hit me, hit me. Otherwise, back the fuck off.

(Prison Guard enters.)

GUARD: Hey, hey.

(Undine, surprised by her own bravado, bursts into tears. The sudden display of emotion catches Inmate #1 off guard, and she backs off. The Prison Guard stares down Undine.)

What's going on in here? Settle down.

(Inmate #2, quiet up until this point, edges toward Undine. She's wearing only one high-heel shoe)

INMATE #2: Don't let her run over you, she born hard. She one of them prehistoric rocks been on the street too long.

(The Prison Guard continues to stare at Undine.)

Hey, sis, don't show him your tears. They get their strength from our pain. You cry the first time, you cry the second time, then the shit don't hurt so much after that. Suck it up.

(The Guard leaves. Undine collects herself.)

What's your name, sis?
UNDINE: . . . Undine.
INMATE #2: That's a pretty name. For a minute you looked like this stuck-up bitch who used to live in my building, but that diva wouldn't be caught dead here.

(Inmate #2 begins to laugh; Undine manages an ironic smile.)

UNDINE: I'm not from—

INMATE #2: Your first time 'hoing?

UNDINE: NO! No. It was a misunderstanding. I don't really belong here—

INMATE #2: Guess what? I don't belong here, she don't belong here, but we here.

UNDINE: But you don't understand—

INMATE #2: Shit, all I was doing was buying formula for my cousin Leticia's baby over on Myrtle Avenue, right? And this dude was, you know, all up in my panties with his eyes, right? On my shit like he my man. "You don't know me, brother," I told him. But he gonna get all pimp on me, like I's his bitch. Big fat Jay-Z-acting muthafucka. He think he all that 'cause he drivin' a Range Rover in my neighborhood. That don't impress me—show me a pay stub, brother. Show me a college diploma. But this dude is gonna step to my face. I told him, put your hands on me and see what happens.

UNDINE: And?

INMATE #2: Why you think I'm here? I showed the muthafucka the point of my heel and the ball of my fist. *(Demonstratively)* I told him, "I ain't your 'ho. I work from nine to five at Metrotech, my man, don't you look at me like a 'ho, don't you talk to me like a 'ho, don't you disrespect me like a video 'ho." Now, he gonna think twice 'fore he place a hand on another woman. Believe it! People think they know your history 'cause of what you wearing. Well guess what? I introduced him to the feminist movement with the back of my muthafuckin' hand.

INMATE #1: That's right. We don't got to take that shit!

UNDINE: They put you in here for that? It doesn't seem fair.

INMATE #2: Shit ain't fair. I mean, why are you here?

UNDINE *(To audience)*: There is the question. I imagine the blurb in my college alumni magazine: "Undine sends word from Riker's Island where she's enjoying creative writing and leading a prison prayer circle."

(Absorbs the horror of the question) Why are we here?

INMATE #2: You know what you done, you ain't gotta tell me. We do what we gots to do, right?

(Lights shift. The voice of Judge Henderson is heard.)

JUDGE HENDERSON: Undine Barnes Calles. Please step forward. The court of King's County, having found you guilty of the criminal possession of a controlled substance—

UNDINE: Your Honor—

JUDGE HENDERSON: —in the seventh degree, hereby sentences you to six months compulsory drug counseling.

UNDINE: But, Your Honor—

JUDGE HENDERSON: Failure to complete the program will result in a one-year jail sentence.

UNDINE: Oh my God!

(Blackout.)

 ACT TWO

Lights rise on a semi-circle of a diverse collection of recovering drug addicts, who look to a sympathetic counselor for guidance. Undine, sipping a cup of coffee, is seated in the midst of the semi-circle.

ADDICT #I: I miss it. I miss the taste and the smell of cocaine, that indescribable surge of confidence that fills the lungs. The numbness at the tip of my tongue, that sour metallic taste of really good blow.

(The Addicts savor the moment with an audible "Mmm.")

It was perfect, I mean, in the middle of the day I'd excuse myself and slip out of an important faculty meeting, go to the stairwell and suck in fifteen, twenty, thirty dollars' worth of crack.

(The Addicts savor the moment with an audible "Mmm.")

I'd return a few minutes later full of energy, ideas, inspired, and then go teach a course on early American literature and not give a goddamn. In fact, the students admired my bold, gutsy devil-may-care attitude. Why? Because I'd lecture brilliantly and passionately on books . . . I hadn't read. Indeed, the university didn't know how high and mighty I was when they promoted me chair of the English department and gave me an office with a view of Jersey. It was fantastic—I could smoke crack all day, every day in my office, seated in my leather chair, at my solid oak desk. It was near perfect, it was as close to nirvana as a junkie can achieve. But my colleagues were always on my case: "Beep. Mr. Logan wants you to attend a panel on the symbolism of the tomahawk in *The Deerslayer.*" "Beep, Beep. Ms. Cortini is here for her thesis defense, what should I tell her?" Those thesis writing motherfuckers drove me crazy. And I wanted to kill them. But you know what happens, I don't have to tell any of you junkies. "Beep. Sayer wants to see you in his office. Right this minute." "Beep. He's getting impatient." Fuck you! But by that time I was on a four-day binge, my corduroy blazer stank like Chinatown. And I was paraded through the hallowed halls like some pathetic cocaine poster child.

But, I don't remember when I became a criminal, it happened at some point after that. The descent was classic, it's not even worthy of detail. Bla, bla, bla.

(A moment. Guy, a gentle man wearing a security guard uniform, speaks up.)

GUY: But you're clean, son. You're clear.

ADDICT #1: One year. One year clean and I still walk around the city wondering how people cope, how do they survive without the aid of some substance? A boost? It makes me angry—no, envious. How come some people get to lead lives filled with meaning and happiness? And I become a drug-addled junkie scheming for my next fix.

ADDICT #2: Fuck them!

ADDICT #1: Excuse me, I didn't interrupt you. Thank you. And you know what I think? I think that they will never understand the joy and comfort of that very first moment you draw the smoke into your lungs releasing years of stress, of not giving a damn whether you live or die. They won't know what it is to crave and love something so deeply that you're willing to lie, cheat and steal to possess it. They won't know that kind of passion. I accept that I may go to hell, but I've experienced a kind of surrender, a letting go of self that years of meditation and expensive yuppie yoga classes won't yield. And I hold on to that feeling, fiendishly. That feeling empowers me, because I know the Shaolin strength that it takes to resist it, to fight it, to defeat it.

(A chorus of agreement rises up.)

UNDINE *(To audience)*: The perversity of this moment is that, in the midst of his loathsome confession, I'm actually finding myself strangely curious to smoke crack cocaine. I have now concluded that for every addict that the system cures, two new ones are created.

COUNSELOR: Undine, you've been sitting quietly, is there anything you want to share?

UNDINE: Other than: "The only meaningful contact I have these days is with the first sips of coffee in the morning"? No. I'll just listen today.

COUNSELOR: You've been here five weeks. I think it might be helpful to open up.

ADDICTS: Open up, open up. *(They applaud in agreement)*

UNDINE *(To audience)*: Oh, to share my addictions. To confess to the stack of fashion magazines that I keep in my bathroom like some treasured porn collection, which I read and reread with utter salacious delight. No, I won't share that. Instead I manufacture some elaborate tale of addiction. I've decided to use Percodan as my gateway drug. And I concoct a tale so pathetically moving that I am touched by my own invention, and regret not having experienced the emotions firsthand. But the tears are genuine. I am crying. And I weep, and I'm applauded by the room of addicts, and it is exhilarating. A rush. And I understand addiction.

(Undine breaks down in tears. She is comforted by the Addicts.)

COUNSELOR: Remember this room is a safe haven. Whatever is spoken within this circle remains within the circle. And that trust is sacred as long as the circle is unbroken.

UNDINE: I'm pregnant and I don't know whether I want this child.

GUY: It is a blessing to be faced with such a dilemma.

UNDINE: What?

GUY: I said it's a blessing to be faced with such a dilemma.

UNDINE: Why?

GUY: A child, a possibility, a lesson.

UNDINE *(To audience)*: He is speaking in sentence fragments and I find him curiously intriguing. *(To Guy)* And?

GUY: 'Cause.

UNDINE: Yeah?

GUY: You know.

UNDINE: What?

GUY: A baby.

UNDINE: Yes?

GUY: Is a beautiful thing. *(Smiles)* Not all of us have so perfect a reason to stay straight.

UNDINE: Oh my. You're right.

GUY: How long have you been using?

UNDINE: Long enough.

GUY: I've been clean for two years, it's my anniversary tonight and I'm trying to figure out how to celebrate. Will you have dinner with me?

UNDINE: Are you asking me out on a date?

GUY: Yes.

UNDINE *(To audience)*: Dinner with a junkie? If I were a poet I would go home and compose a poem, threading the bits of irony through the improbability, but I'm not, so I say yes. BBQ on St. Marks and Second, a place I've shunned for a decade. He is reformed, he is magnificent and he is paying the bill.

(They sit side by side in the restaurant.)

GUY: I considered going into corrections, but a life of policing people behind bars seemed too, you know—

UNDINE: Depressing.

GUY: Yeah. It's like all my friends, they either in jail, they on they way to jail or they the brothers watching the brothers in jail. I don't want that. It ain't part of my schedule. I'm clean, my head's like in the right place. I've been working at the Cineplex as a security guard, and I'm gonna take the firemen's exam next month.

UNDINE: A fireman, that's wonderful.

GUY: I got good upper body strength—

UNDINE: I bet you do.

GUY: And I can withstand really high temperatures, since I was eleven. It's one of those things. I'm studying in the evenings. And this time next year I'll be a fireman.

UNDINE: Really, I believe you will.

GUY: Yeah? You think so?

UNDINE: You know, I had my own business, a public relations firm. It started in a restaurant over a glass of wine. I had an expression very much like yours. I went from employee to entrepreneur between dinner and dessert. Really.

(Guy laughs.)

GUY: I knew that about you. I knew that when you was sitting there quietly in counseling. I was right, wasn't I? You got it going on. I'd like to see you again.

UNDINE: Why?

GUY: 'Cause I dig you.

UNDINE: You dig me? I am dug. You are seeing me on a good day. You're seeing me way out of context.

GUY: Well, I'm liking what I see.

UNDINE: Oh, so you're going to get smooth? That's okay, bring it. But be warned, I am not an easy person.

GUY: That's cool, but can I see you again?

UNDINE: No, I don't think so. I don't think it's such a good idea.

GUY: Why not?

UNDINE: I can't be with a man in uniform.

GUY *(Seductively)*: What about a brother out of uniform?

UNDINE: In case you forgot, I'm pregnant.

GUY: So? I think you're brave to make a go of this alone. I got mad respect for you, battling dope, walking the straight and narrow.

UNDINE: It isn't an act of bravery, let me clear that up right now. I didn't plan for this to happen. It is a by-product of an unholy union.

GUY: And a blessing, no doubt.

UNDINE: You don't let up. You are going to give this a positive spin if it kills you.

GUY: I guess I'm that kinda brother. And I dig that you didn't laugh when I told you about, you know, what I want to do.

(Undine stands up.)

UNDINE *(To audience)*: His sincerity is sickening. He has none of Hervé's charm, which makes him all the more charming. Flash forward: a fireman, with a pension and a tacky three-bedroom in Syosset, Long Island. Flashback: Hervé.

(Hervé, exquisitely attired, appears.)

HERVÉ: Corfu, Milano, Barcelona, Rio.

UNDINE *(To audience)*: I am—

(Guy and Hervé retreat into the darkness. Two women in their mid-thirties appear.)

SCENE 2

The courtyard of the Walt Whitman projects. Rosa pushes a stroller. She wears a BabyBjörn baby carrier, which holds an infant. Devora is ghetto fabulous.

 Undine puts on her sunglasses, trying to avoid contact. She attempts to flee, but:

ROSA *(Shouts)*: SHARONA WATKINS. Sharona!

DEVORA: That can't—

ROSA: Yes, it is.

DEVORA: Oh no, no.

(Undine can't hide.)

ROSA: Oh hell, somebody told me it was you. But I was, like, what?
UNDINE: Hey.
DEVORA: Hey?
ROSA: You don't remember us, do you?
UNDINE: I'm sorry.

ROSA *(Sings)*:
>Down, down baby . . .

ROSA AND DEVORA *(Sing)*:
>Down by the roller coaster,
>Sweet, sweet baby,
>I'll never let you go.
>Shimmy shimmy cocoa pop, shimmy, shimmy pop,
>Kissed my boyfriend.

(Undine, remembering, joins in:)

ROSA, DEVORA AND UNDINE *(Sing)*:
>Naughty, naughty
>Won't do the dishes.
>Lazy, Lazy,
>Stole a piece of candy.
>Greedy, greedy,
>Jumped off a building.
>Crazy, crazy . . .

(The women laugh.)

UNDINE: The Double Dutch Twins.
DEVORA: Rosa Ojeda and Devora Williams.
UNDINE: Oh my God. How are you both?
ROSA: I got a little big, but that's what four children and a husband on disability will do.

DEVORA *(To her sister)*: Don't lie. *(To Undine)* She's big because—

ROSA *(To her sister)*: You don't want me to talk about you.

DEVORA *(To Undine)*: So, mama. What's up?

UNDINE: I'm . . . I'm visiting with my parents, while—

DEVORA: For real? How's that fine brother of yours?

UNDINE: He's all right.

DEVORA: Tell him Devora from 2G said hello. He'll know what you're talking about. Hey!

UNDINE *(To audience)*: Rosa and Devora were the reigning Double Dutch champions in junior high school, but they were eventually beaten by six Japanese girls from Kyoto at Madison Square Garden. It was a crushing blow.

ROSA: I called out to you the other day, but you ain't see me.

UNDINE: I'm sorry. I'm like, you know, dealing with a lot. What are you up to?

ROSA: Not much, you know, the same old, same old. Finally living in building 10, been on the list for seven years. I got me a dope view of Manhattan.

UNDINE: Building 10, no kidding. Congratulations. And Devora? Are you still living in 4?

DEVORA: Oh no. I just bought a brownstone in Fort Greene. I'm a senior financial planner at JPMorgan. I come around once in a while. You know, to see my girl Rosa. And you?

(A moment.)

UNDINE: . . . I'm, um, pregnant and trying—

DEVORA: I bet it's tough, Sharona—

UNDINE: Actually, my name is—

ROSA: That's right, I hear you changed your name to Queen?

UNDINE: No, Undine.

DEVORA: Undine, funny, like that public relations exec, Undine Barnes Calles?

UNDINE: I—

(Gregory, a stylish African American man, dressed for success, enters.)

DEVORA: Pity what happened to her. I hate to see a sister get hurt. I hear she was quite a remarkable diva, but got a little lost. You probably don't even know who I'm talking about.

GREGORY: Honey!

DEVORA: Oh, there's my husband, Gregory. Anyway, it was great seeing you.

(Gregory waves to the women. Devora starts to leave but turns back.)

Listen, I'm starting a financial planning program for underprivileged women. Rosa has joined us. I'd love for you to stop by. Here's my card.

UNDINE *(To audience)*: And as she thrusts the tricolor card into my hand, it gives me a slight paper cut, just enough to draw blood.

DEVORA: Call me.

UNDINE *(To audience)*: And she means it.

(Devora and Gregory leave.)

ROSA: She's doing it! And folks like us are just left to sit back and marvel.

UNDINE: But I—

ROSA: I know. Me, too. So, when are you due, mama?

UNDINE: Oh no, you don't understand, I'm not having this baby. No. I just didn't realize it was so hard to find a "reasonably" priced clinic in this city, to you know—

ROSA: Girl, I got two words for you: social services. It's the Amen at the end of my day.

(Lights rise on a Department of Social Services office. A line of exhausted people has formed.)

UNDINE *(To audience)*: Social services. The poor man's penance. The most dreaded part of the system.

SCENE 3

Department of Social Services. An impatient Caseworker with long airbrushed nails cradles a phone receiver in her hand, while doing her best to ignore the ever-growing group of people waiting in the endless line. Undine approaches the Caseworker and taps on her desk. An illegible sign hangs behind her head reading: Please ill out he orm.

CASEWORKER: You don't know how to fill out a form?
UNDINE: I didn't know there was even a form to be filled out.
CASEWORKER: What do the sign say?
UNDINE: Please ill out he orm.
CASEWORKER: So what do that tell you?
UNDINE: Nothing intelligible.
CASEWORKER: Fill this out and come back.
UNDINE: Do I have to wait in line again?
CASEWORKER: Yeah. Next.
UNDINE: But I have already been waiting in line for two hours.
CASEWORKER: Yeah and? I can't do nothing for you until the form's filled out.
UNDINE: Maybe it might be helpful if you let people know that they have to fill out the form before they get to you.
CASEWORKER: Maybe. Next.
UNDINE: Wait. Do I fill out both sides or just the front?
CASEWORKER: Listen, you can rap to me all day, but I ain't like all y'all, I got work to do. NEXT.
UNDINE *(To audience)*: So I meticulously fill out the form.
    Two hideous hours later:

(The people move in a circular line until it is Undine's turn again. Undine walks up to the Caseworker, who is on the phone.)

There you go. I was wondering how quickly medical benefits will kick in—you see I'm in a time-sensitive situation—
CASEWORKER: Well, this ain't the right form.
UNDINE: This is the form you gave me.

CASEWORKER: You sure I gave it to you?

UNDINE: Yes.

CASEWORKER: Well, I can't do nothing for you unless you fill out the right form. Next.

UNDINE: Wait just one moment.

PERSON IN LINE: Come on!

UNDINE: What form do I need?

CASEWORKER: 7001.

UNDINE: Which form is this?

CASEWORKER: 7002.

UNDINE: Do you have form 7001?

CASEWORKER *(Into the phone)*: Hold on, girl. *(Exasperated, she slams down the phone. Shouts)* Lance, you got any more of form 7001 back there?

LANCE *(From offstage)*: Yes!

CASEWORKER: Bring 'em!

UNDINE: This is crazy. I've been standing in this heat and I—

(Lance enters. He hands the Caseworker a pile of forms.)

CASEWORKER: You're gonna fill this out and get back in line when you're done. *(Starts to hand Undine the form)*

UNDINE *(Interrupting)*: Excuse me? I'm not waiting another two hours in that line.

CASEWORKER: Then come back first thing tomorrow morning. Next.

WOMAN IN LINE *(To Undine)*: Don't get too upset. They always like this. I filled out four forms and spent three days here last month. And still ain't got no further than the front desk. In actuality, I don't think there is anything beyond this point. I think that they like to give you the illusion that they can help—keep us busy so we forget that they ain't doing nothing for us.

UNDINE: But don't you want to see what's in the next room?

WOMAN IN LINE: See what's in the next room? *(She and the other people in line laugh ironically)* Good luck . . . Send word if you get to the promised land.

UNDINE *(To Caseworker)*: I demand to speak to your supervisor.

CASEWORKER: I am the supervisor, what you got to say?

(A moment.)

UNDINE: Oh? You're the supervisor? Can I say, this whole thing is not being handled professionally. You're rude, and you treat people like cattle. You don't know what circumstances brought each of us here. We've waited all day to get to this point, we just want to sit in a room and talk to somebody, anybody. I mean, isn't there anyone in all this miserable bureaucracy who isn't merely concerned with what time to take lunch? We need help. We're entitled to this benefit. We've all humbled ourselves just by being here and you're behaving like some centurion guarding the gates to Rome. I mean, who gave you the right to condescend.

CASEWORKER: And you know what else? We just ran out of the form you need.

UNDINE: He just handed you a pile of forms.

CASEWORKER: So? You think you're entitled to some special treatment. Guess what? I ain't giving you shit. Step out of line until you can stand correct. Next!

WOMAN IN LINE *(To Undine)*: Oh no, baby, I wouldn't make her angry if I were you.

UNDINE *(Unhinged)*: GIVE ME THE MUTHAFUCKING FORM!

CASEWORKER: Miss, I'll have you medically removed from the building.

UNDINE: I'm not leaving without the form. *(Chanting)* Give us the form. We want the form. *(Urges the others on, rallying the troops)* Come on, people! Give us the form! Give us the form!

CROWD *(Chanting)*: We want the form! We want the form! We want the form!

UNDINE: We can come back tomorrow and start this whole damn process again. But who wins?

CROWD: Yeah!

CASEWORKER: NEXT!

UNDINE *(To audience)*: And I am medically removed from the building, which means the paramedics arrive, administer a mild sedative, strap me to a gurney and rush me to the nearest psychiatric facility. I spend a half hour speaking to a gentle intern who incidentally went to college with my assistant, Stephie, and I am subsequently released with a prescription for a powerful antipsychotic . . . which I can't use because I'm pregnant. And after all of that I still must go back to the office the next morning to fill out form 7001. And after weeks of agony and bureaucratic hell I was finally able to see a doctor.

(Lights rise on a waiting room in a public medical clinic.)

SCENE 4

We're in a waiting room. A very Young Pregnant Woman sits down next to Undine. The woman noisily sips on a can of grape soda. Undine tries hard to ignore her. Finally:

YOUNG PREGNANT WOMAN: Twins. A boy and girl. The jackpot first time around. What about you?

UNDINE: First.

YOUNG PREGNANT WOMAN: Your first? Really? But you're so old.

UNDINE: But you're so young. *(A moment. To audience)* Surely, I don't look that old, do I? *(To the woman)* I'm just thirty-seven.

YOUNG PREGNANT WOMAN: Wow. You're my mother's age.

UNDINE: Your mother is thirty-seven?

 (To audience) I say nothing, though I want to let her know that I don't belong here, that my life experience is rich and textured and not represented well in this low, coarse clinic lighting. As such, I show her a touch of condescension, perhaps even pity. *(Displays a touch of condescension)*

 (To audience) But I'm panicking. *(The young pregnant woman looks at Undine)* And I look at her and I realize, she's looking back at me with a touch of condescension. Pity, even. And we both look away. *(They both look away)*

YOUNG PREGNANT WOMAN: My boyfriend is in Iraq.

UNDINE *(To audience)*: I wish she hadn't told me. *(Opens a magazine)*

YOUNG PREGNANT WOMAN: I started—

UNDINE *(To audience)*: She wants to talk, I pretend not to hear her.

YOUNG PREGNANT WOMAN: We were planning to move out of the—

UNDINE *(To herself)*: Please, Doctor, call me in. Call me in before Edna returns, I'm having trouble breathing.

YOUNG PREGNANT WOMAN: I hadn't planned on getting—

UNDINE *(To herself)*: Stop! I can't breathe.

YOUNG PREGNANT WOMAN: I'm scared.

(A moment. Undine reaches out and uncharacteristically takes the Young Pregnant Woman's hand.)

UNDINE: I'm scared, too.

(Undine's breathing becomes labored. Anxiety. The lights shift and we're in the Doctor's office.)

DOCTOR: Ms. Calles.

(Undine stands.)

UNDINE: Yes.

DOCTOR *(Cold and indifferent)*: Judging from the size of the fetus, I'd predict that you're a little further along than you say.

UNDINE: How much further?

DOCTOR: You're six and a half months.

UNDINE: No, no I can't possibly be that far along.

DOCTOR: That's a conservative estimate. *(The Doctor speaks slowly, adopting a patronizing, pedagogical tone)* I can't impress upon new mothers enough the importance of prenatal care to the health of the fetus. Do you understand what I'm saying?

UNDINE: Doctor, English is my first language, you don't have to speak to me like an idiot. Get to the point.

DOCTOR: Ms. Calles, you really should have come in sooner.

UNDINE: Listen, I tried to make an appointment with my regular doctor, but she wouldn't see me without health insurance. I attempted to make an appointment with another gynecologist, but it seems I needed a referral from the local clinic. I went to the local clinic, but I didn't have the appropriate paperwork. Apparently when I became poor I was no longer worthy of good health care. Doctor, all I want is an—

DOCTOR: If you give this form to the nurse she'll set up your next ultrasound appointment.

UNDINE: No, no, no. You don't understand. I'm not having this baby. No, no, no. I'm not a mother-to-be. Okay. I am not a parent. What can be done?

DOCTOR: At this stage, nothing. You're too far along.

UNDINE: Yeah, but what can be done?

DOCTOR: Eat right and take good care of yourself. Here's a prescription for prenatal vitamins. I'll see you in a month. *(The Doctor hands Undine the prescription)* Oh, Ms. Calles, would you like to hear the baby's heartbeat before you leave?

UNDINE *(Shocked)*: What?

DOCTOR: Many women like—

UNDINE: No . . . yes. I'm not sure. *(A moment)* Doctor.

DOCTOR: Yes?

UNDINE: Do you think the baby knows what I'm feeling?

DOCTOR: I don't know. But I like to think so.

(A moment. The Doctor exits. Undine sits, frozen. She looks at the prescription.)

UNDINE *(Contemplating; to audience)*: Optimox prenatal tabs? I go to Duane Reade on the Upper West Side of Manhattan; it's like a vacation wandering the well-stocked aisles of the pharmacy tended by employees in pristine uniforms.

(Lights shift. We're in Duane Reade. Pleasant music plays in the background.)

SCENE 5

Duane Reade. A young woman, dressed in a uniform, busies herself stocking items on a shelf.

UNDINE: Miss. I'm looking for calcium tablets and vitamins.

(Stephie, startled, turns around in her pharmacy uniform.)

Stephie?
STEPHIE: Undine?

(They gawk at each other.)

UNDINE: What are—
STEPHIE: This is only temporary. Actually I'm interviewing like crazy. I've come really close to several things. God, look at you.
UNDINE: Look at you.
STEPHIE: I tried to call you last month for a recommendation, but—
UNDINE: I've moved to Brooklyn.
STEPHIE: Great.
UNDINE: It's great.
STEPHIE: Great.
UNDINE: Great.

(A moment.)

STEPHIE: This is about paying a few bills. I'm told it's like important to have all kinds of experiences.
UNDINE: True.
STEPHIE: Man. How far along are you?
UNDINE: Almost seven months.
STEPHIE: You with a baby. *(Gives off a little laugh)*
UNDINE: Why is that funny to you?
STEPHIE: I don't know. I'm sorry, but you always seemed like—
UNDINE: Like what?
STEPHIE: I don't know. Like. *(A moment)* Never mind.
UNDINE: The calcium pills are in which aisle?
STEPHIE: Seven—no, no, four. I'm trying not to get used to this. I don't really want to know where things are, because once you do, you're sorta committed. Right? This is just temporary.
LOUDSPEAKER: Stephie, you're needed in aisle two, for stacking.
STEPHIE: Oh God, they're calling me. I'm like the stock guru. If I really wanted to, I could be Employee of the Month, every month.

But there's nothing worse than bad blood between minimum-wage workers. I'm not trying to go there.

LOUDSPEAKER: Stephie, you're needed in aisle two. Pronto!

STEPHIE: Coming! Like nothing changes. I gotta run.

UNDINE: Go.

(Stephie turns to leave.)

STEPHIE: Hey, Undine. *(No response)* Undine! Are you happy?

(Undine turns away.)

UNDINE *(To audience)*: I want to turn back, but I don't. I do not answer. I slip the calcium tablets into my pocket, unpaid, and I keep walking. I walk all the way home fighting a tinge of envy, because Stephie, my former assistant, might actually be named Employee of the Month at the pharmacy.

(Crossfade to the Walt Whitman projects.)

SCENE 6

Kitchen. The table has chairs propped on top. Flow and Mother, as usual, are dressed in their security guard uniforms. Grandma is crocheting a doily. Mother, with a word search puzzle book tucked in her back pocket, sweeps the floor. Flow is in the midst of an animated story. Undine, ankles swollen, navigates the kitchen table, struggling to open a childproof bottle of pills.

FLOW: And I took the shoplifter to the back of the store and gave him my Nelson Mandela speech. I said, "The African brother gave up twenty-eight years of freedom for his ideals, for his principles, for the struggle to liberate black Africans from the griplock of apartheid." I said, "Little brother thief, liberating a box of lubricated super-strong Trojans ain't a reason to go to jail. Don't let the system fuck you because you're horny. If you're going to give up your damn freedom, make sure it's for a just cause." And, Ma, I saw a little something in his eyes, a spark, a touch of recognition, and I quickly unfastened his handcuffs. And then this little fool is gonna ask, "Who Nelson Mandela?" I had to slap homeboy out of his chair and call 911. Shit, there ain't no greater crime than abandoning your history.

MOTHER: That's right.

(Undine is breathing heavily, struggling with the pills.)

UNDINE: Hello, could someone give me hand?

MOTHER: Flow!

(Flow helps Undine open the pills.)

FLOW: Damn, girl, you getting big.

UNDINE: What-ever.

FLOW: What's your problem?

UNDINE *(Snapping)*: I'm having a fucking baby!

(Undine slaps the bottle of pills on the table.)

FLOW: No shit, when'd you realize that? Sharona!

UNDINE: Ty-rell!

FLOW: Here's a little something for the baby daddy.

(Flow does a series of elaborate tricks with his nightstick. Undine grabs the club and tosses it on the table.)

UNDINE: By the way, how's the epic poem coming?

(Flow suddenly grows somber.)

MOTHER: You two are acting like teenagers. Stop it! —Oh Undine, somebody called for you while you were at the doctor's office.

UNDINE: Who?

FLOW: Did you tell them there ain't no Undine living here?

UNDINE: That's getting old. Okay?

FLOW: What's the matter with you?

UNDINE: My life is not exactly going as I planned. "Aw'right?" Mom, did the phone call sound important?

MOTHER: I don't know, what does important sound like?

UNDINE *(To audience)*: A pardon. Absolution. My life back. Was it Hervé calling from Barbados to say: "Join me"? Would I? Oh, would I.

MOTHER: I'm sure they'll call back.

(Father, seemingly tired, enters wearing his security uniform.)

FLOW: Hey there. What's the word, Pop?

FATHER: Walking the walk.

MOTHER: Hope you didn't forget the lotto tickets . . . Don't tell me you forgot.

FATHER: I forgot? *(Excited)* I ain't forget.

(Father passes out the lotto tickets to his family. He gives Mother a kiss on the head.)

The lotto line ran around the block. Stood, twenty-five minutes. Junie got heself one hundred tickets, he thinks this time he gonna be lucky 'cause Clarice momma had a dream about fish. *(They all gasp with excitement)* But he doesn't want to share his luck with anybody, jack.

UNDINE: Excuse me, I don't mean to interrupt this precious moment, but Mom, was it a man that called?

MOTHER: Did she really dream about fish?

FLOW: When that woman dream fish, money fall out the sky?

UNDINE: Fish?

FLOW: Don't you know, girl?

GRANDMA *(Suddenly)*: It means good fortune coming your way, sweet pea.

MOTHER *(To Undine, remembering)*: Oh that's right, it was a man that called, Grandma said—

UNDINE: You let him speak to Grandma?

MOTHER: I had a pot of gumbo about to burn on the stove.

FATHER: You made your gumbo?

UNDINE (*Exasperated*): Grandma, was it my accountant? Was it . . . Hervé?

GRANDMA: Who's Hervé?

UNDINE: He's my husband. What did the man say? It's very important! (*Shouts*) I need to know!

FLOW: Don't you yell at her! She's an old woman! She's got diabetes, damn it.

UNDINE: Flow, she doesn't have diabetes. For God's sake, she's a junkie—a junkie! I've been taking her to the methadone clinic for a month.

(*It's a ridiculous notion to all but Undine.*)

Hello! People! (*Shouts*) Is anybody home?

MOTHER: Why are you so upset? It's just a phone call. If it's important the person will call back.

UNDINE: It isn't the phone call! It's . . . It's a phantom poem that won't ever be completed, it's thousands of dollars of lotto tickets that should have been invested in the stock market, it's a thrown-away solution and, Mom, when are you going to stop searching for words? It's the fact that Grandma is a—

GRANDMA: Oh lawd, she's carry low. It makes some people crazy in the third trimester.

UNDINE: Aren't you listening to what I'm saying? Are you blind and deaf? Or are we just going to sit around all day and talk about fish?

(*A moment. Flow suddenly jumps up.*)

FLOW (*Furious passion*):
    This ain't the beginnin' you wuz expectin'
    It ain't a poem, but a reckonin'
    Be it sacred or profane,
    Or a divine word game.
    It all about a rabbit,
    Or it ain't.

It ain't a holler or a song.
It ain't no geechie folk yawn.
It ain't a road that been tread,
With a stained rag around the head.
It all about a rabbit,
Or it ain't.

It ain't a myth that so old,
That it been whole-saled and re-sold.
It ain't a Bible lover's tale
Or a preacher's parting wail.

Wait. Wait. Okay. Here we go.
It all about a rabbit,
Or it ain't.

'Cuz.

It that ghetto paradox,
When we rabbit and we fox,
And we basking in the blight
Though we really wanna fight.

It 'bout who we be today,
And in our fabulating way
'Bout saying that we be
Without a-pology.
It's a circle that been run
That ain't no one ever won.
It that silly rabbit grin
'Bout running from your skin,

'Cuz.

It a . . . It a . . .

MOTHER *(Coaxing Flow)*: C'mon. C'mon.

FLOW:

It a . . . It a . . . It a—

(Flow stops mid-sentence as abruptly as he began, struggling to find the next word in the poem. The family is as anxious to find it as he is.)

FATHER: Don't stop, don't stop—

FLOW: It a . . .

MOTHER: C'mon.

FLOW *(Frustrated)*: It ain't finished. It ain't done till it's done. A fabulation takes time. It doesn't just happen.

UNDINE: A fabulation? Yeah, but how long, Flow?

FLOW: I don't know, fourteen years and nine months. You tell me. And what do you care? We died in a fire.

(A moment.)

UNDINE *(To audience)*: It was an unforeseen tragedy, really. A misprint.

FLOW: What, you didn't think we saw the article?

MOTHER: *Black Enterprise*, page thirty-eight, article continued on ninety-one.

FATHER: You see we ain't totally blind. We read.

MOTHER: It was a very good article, Undine. We were very proud of you, until the part where they said your family died in a fire. Baby, we didn't die in a fire.

UNDINE: Yes, I know that. I was apparently misquoted.

FLOW: A misquote?

MOTHER: That's what I told your father. You see, baby. I told him that. We're your family. I said, she's done many things, but she'd never do that!

FATHER: Is that true . . . Undine?

UNDINE: Surely, you can't believe everything you read.

FATHER: Is that true . . . Undine?

GRANDMA: 'Cause you know the Watkins family is there inside you. And we love it, even if . . . This *is* your home.

FATHER: Is it *true* . . . Undine?

FLOW: Why?

UNDINE *(To audience)*: Is this it? Is this the end of the story? A dramatic family confrontation. Catharsis. Is it that simple? A journey that began miraculously at the Walt Whitman projects and led me to Edith Wharton's *The Custom of the Country*, an intriguing parvenu discovered in an American Literature course at Dartmouth College.

(A moment.)

No. No. I go to a street corner with a twenty-dollar bill balled up in my fist. I buy twenty dollars' worth of white lace. I take it to the stairwell. I really must have angered Elegba, I must have unsettled all of the powerful orishas. And I'm ready to surrender, I'm ready to concede, I'm so ready. And just as I'm about . . . they unexpectedly find Hervé.

(A prison waiting room.)

SCENE 7

Hervé slowly emerges from the darkness, wearing a bright orange prison uniform; he moves with grace. Undine sits across from him at the visitor's table.

UNDINE *(To audience)*: They found him hiding out at the Ritz-Carlton, pretending to be a diplomat from Uruguay. Unfortunately for him a diplomat from Uruguay was also a guest at the hotel, attending a summit on global warming.

(Hervé points to her bulging stomach.)

HERVÉ: What happened to you?
UNDINE: What do you think happened to me?
HERVÉ: Who did this to you?
UNDINE: You did, you fucker!

HERVÉ: Me?

UNDINE: Yes.

(A moment.)

HERVÉ: How?

UNDINE: How do you think?

HERVÉ: Oh yes, I see.

(A moment.)

UNDINE: Why?

HERVÉ: Why not?

UNDINE: All of it?

HERVÉ: It happened, *si*. It is finished.

UNDINE: I could kill you. I cared for you, you little prick. And you didn't even have the decency to say good-bye.

HERVÉ: I am sorry.

UNDINE: You can take your "sorry" to federal prison.

HERVÉ: Let us talk.

UNDINE: I have nothing to say to you. My lawyer will speak for me. You took everything from me.

HERVÉ: Not everything. My father's name was Javier Dejesus Calles. He was a good man. I offer you his name, it is the name for my son, for my daughter.

UNDINE: Well, that won't do.

HERVÉ: But, I am the father of your child.

UNDINE: Oh please, you were fucking for a green card—that's enough to keep any Latin dick hard. *(A moment)* You are the father, but you won't be this child's father. You left our lives, you gave up your parental rights as far as I'm concerned. I was generous to you, I was more than generous.

HERVÉ: I beg your pardon, *querida*, you were generous to nobody. I disappeared long before I left, but you just never noticed. Money? You'll make more money. Don't pretend it was about the money.

UNDINE: Oh please.

HERVÉ: I pity the child.

UNDINE: Why would you say that?

HERVÉ: I think you understand, Undine. *(Undine stares at Hervé)* I was open, but you are a rotten oyster. We look at each other—now. It is the first time we stand face-to-face since we met, no? I am who I was, *querida*, you are who you were. We are ugly people. We give, we take, we are even.

UNDINE *(To audience)*: I've prided myself on not needing love, but it was different when I thought I was loved.

HERVÉ: Guard.

(Hervé leaves.)

UNDINE *(Resigned)*: Hervé!
    (To audience) And he is gone. But strangely I dream of fish.

(The sound of the ocean. Undine is surrounded by the group of Addicts.)

SCENE 8

The Addicts, including Guy, sit in a support circle. Undine enters.

ADDICT #2: Old friends, old friends. I shouldn't have rode in the car with my old friends. They were smoking herb and I thought, A little herb won't kill me.

COUNSELOR: Take a moment. We're not here to judge, this is a place of forgiveness. Take your time.

(Addict #2 begins to weep. Undine walks over to the coffee-and-tea cart. She lets out a loud involuntary gasp caused by a slight contraction.)

Are you okay, Undine?

UNDINE: Yes. I'm sorry.

(Guy breaks away from the circle and goes over to Undine. In a whisper, Guy and Undine carry on their own conversation. The group continues its work.)

GUY: Did you get my telephone message?

UNDINE: You? No.

GUY: No? Have you begun your birthing classes?

UNDINE: I haven't even thought that far ahead.

GUY: Don't you think maybe you better?

UNDINE: Yes. I suppose eventually I will have to give birth.

GUY: If you need someone to go with you to the classes, I'd be glad.

UNDINE: That's okay.

COUNSELOR *(Rising)*: Was there something you wish to share with the group, Undine?

UNDINE: Oh no. I'm just getting a cup of tea.

(Addict #2 continues to speak in the background:)

ADDICT #2: The radio was pumping, the feeling was familiar. Two hits, what's the harm? *(A collective groan)*

(Guy and Undine continue to whisper.)

GUY: Really, if you need a partner, someone to be in the delivery room with you. I know we don't know each other that well, but I'd be happy to be that person that, you know, who stands by you in the delivery room.

UNDINE: Really?

GUY: Yeah.

UNDINE: You'll hold my hand? Breathe in and out with me?

GUY: I'm serious.

UNDINE: Yes, I know that you're serious. And you're so sweet. But, would you really? Oh my God, this is going to happen.

GUY: You'll be fine. You ain't like the other addicts in this program. I mean you seem . . . stronger.

UNDINE *(To audience)*: But he doesn't know that Edna is pressing gently against my chest, slowly quickening my breath, squeezing. *(Touches her swollen belly)* Or that I feel the child kicking my side, and I hate that my body is not mine alone.

(Guy, smiling, gently places his hand on Undine's belly.)

GUY: Hey.

UNDINE: Why are you smiling?

GUY: You.

UNDINE: What?

GUY: You know.

UNDINE: Yes?

GUY: Look beautiful.

UNDINE: No. Don't say that.

GUY: Why? You make me happy. It has been a struggle, no doubt, but when I think about what's happened to me in the last few months, it's all good, for real. You.

Two years ago I was living on the street. I'd see my moms, my boys and they'd pretend not to know me. I was starving, and they'd walk right by me. Ashamed. Yeah, I been that person. I been that brother you cross the street to avoid, I been wrong at times, I been to jail for six months. But that's over, never again. I let go of the bullshit. I hope you know that.

Why do you look confused?

UNDINE: I've never heard anyone say they're happy and actually feel it. But when you say it, I'm looking at you, I believe you mean it. And I find that reassuring.

(The Addicts slowly shift their attention to Undine and Guy, who are still standing by the coffee-and-tea cart.)

GUY: Why?

UNDINE: Because mostly I feel rage.

(Undine realizes the Addicts are eavesdropping and finds herself including them in her confessional.)

Anger, which I guess is a variation of rage and sometimes it gives way to panic, which in my case is also a variation of rage. I think it's safe to say that I've explored the full range of rage.

ADDICTS: Mmm.

UNDINE: And it has been with me for so long, that it's comforting. I'm trying to move beyond it—sometimes I even think I have—but mostly I'm not a very good human being. Sometimes I'm less than human, I know this, but I can't control it. And now I'm more afraid than ever.

GUY: Why?

UNDINE: Because, what if I'm not a good enough person to be a parent?

GUY: Of course you are.

UNDINE: No! I'm not! I killed my family. *(A collective gasp)* Yes, I killed all of them on the day of my college graduation. Dartmouth. My family drove two hundred and sixty-seven miles in a rented minivan, loaded with friends and relatives eager to witness my ceremony. They were incredibly proud, and why not? I was the first person in the family to graduate from college. They came en masse, dressed in their bargain-basement finest. Loud, overly eager, lugging picnic baskets filled with fragrant ghetto food . . . let's just say their enthusiasm overwhelmed me. But I didn't mind, no, I didn't mind until I overheard a group of my friends making crass, unkind comments about my family. They wondered aloud who belonged to *those* people. It was me. I should have said so. I should have said that my mother took an extra shift so I could have a new coat every year. My father sent me ten dollars every week, his lotto money. But instead I locked myself in my dorm room and refused to come out to greet them. And I decided on that day that I was Undine Barnes, who bore no relationship to those people. I told everyone my family died in a fire, and I came to accept it as true. And it was true for years. Understand, Sharona had to die in a fire in order for Undine to live. At least that's what I thought. What I did was awful, and I'm so so sorry. And, Guy, you are such a good, decent man. And I wouldn't blame you if you walked away right now. But I don't want you to.

GUY: Then I won't.

UNDINE: I am not yet divorced, I'm being investigated by the FBI, I'm carrying the child of another man, and I'm not really a junkie.
    (A collective gasp from the Addicts)
        (To Guy) Are you still happy?

GUY: Yes. I think so.

UNDINE: And you're not medicated?

GUY: No.

UNDINE: Give us a moment.

(A moment. The group turns away. Undine pulls Guy aside.)

Is the notion of love frightening to you?

GUY: No.

UNDINE: Who are you? Why are you doing this to me? I'm sorry, I didn't mean to say that, I take it back. I mean, I like you a great deal—love is heavy, is deep and frightening, and I apologize for floating it so carelessly. I really want to change, I do, but I'm afraid I can't. I'm not ready for this.

GUY: Stop. Stop speaking.

(Guy leans in and plants a kiss on Undine's lips; she surrenders. A labor pain hits. The Addicts gasp and collectively back away.
Lights slowly shift to the hospital room.)

SCENE 9

Guy and the Doctor help Undine onto an examining table. Bright, unforgiving light.

UNDINE *(To audience)*: A child? *(Panic)* My child—

(Guy smiles. A pain strikes, interrupting Undine's words.)

GUY: Breathe.

(Undine lies down on the table.)

UNDINE *(To audience)*: Everyone wants me to breathe out, push, but I'm trying desperately to hold my breath, hold it in. If I don't breathe then the baby will not come. *(Holds her breath)*

GUY: Breathe, Undine.

UNDINE *(To audience, holding her breath as she speaks)*: I am holding my
   breath.

DOCTOR: Breathe.

UNDINE *(To audience)*: I am holding on.

(Undine refuses to breathe. Guy takes her hand.)

GUY: Please, breathe.

UNDINE *(To audience)*: I won't. I won't bring a child into this world.

*(Grandma, Mother, Father and Flow enter wearing their security guard
uniforms.)*

FLOW: Breathe, girl!

MOTHER AND FATHER: Breathe, Undine!

(Undine struggles to hold her breath. She's not going to give in.)

GRANDMA: Breathe, sweet pea!

*(Undine looks at Guy and her family in their uniforms; she studies
their concerned faces.)*

UNDINE *(To audience)*: And then I let go.

(Undine wails, a tremendous release. Silence.)

(To audience) I breathe.

*(A baby cries.
   Blackout.)*

END OF PLAY